100 Ways to Make Money in Your Spare Time, Starting With Less Than $100

100 Ways to Make Money in Your Spare Time, Starting With Less Than $100

John Stockwell
Herbert Holtje

Parker Publishing Company, Inc.   *West Nyack, N.Y.*

LIBRARY OF CONGRESS
CATALOG CARD NUMBER: 70–179452

PRINTED IN THE UNITED STATES OF AMERICA
ISBN–0–13–636522–1
B&P

How This Book
Will Give You a Formula
for Success

We will show you in the following pages how to use a simple formula to build the "Wealth Base" you need to achieve personal prosperity, starting with an initial investment of $100 or less. Many people have used this formula to increase their incomes, and you can, too.

We will introduce you to Harold Grant who, starting with $20, applied these simple success principles during his spare time. In a little over a year he was earning $20,000 a year in his own business, and later sold it for $80,000 cash. His true story is told in Chapter 1.

Let the Stories of Others Be Your Beacon to Wealth. We will give you numerous true-to-life case histories of people who have traveled various roads to wealth. These stories will show you, in down-to-earth fashion:

- how to start a business in your spare time with less than $100
- how to build the security of a second income while you are still working at your present job

- how to pyramid business upon business and income upon income
- how to discover the hard-earned business success secrets of others
- how to exercise your inalienable right to success, personal independence, and wealth

Methods That Work Anywhere, Anytime, and for Anyone. Bernie Callahan was a low-paid clerk in a small Midwestern retail store. Using one of the businesses we describe (*Advertising Distribution Services*), Bernie grossed over $12,000 a year just working on Saturdays.

Doris Williamson was a housewife seeking to supplement her husband's income. With nothing more elaborate than a decent typewriter and some easily-acquired directories, she is earning an average of $600 a month, and works less than two days a week. Her method is detailed under *Prospect List Compilation.*

Tom Harris earned $22,000 the second year after he started a *Drafting Service* business . . . and he wasn't even a draftsman himself!

These and many other businesses used successfully by others are described in the following pages. All you have to do is to follow the step-by-step instructions for building your own Wealth Base.

To benefit fully from the wealth of hard-earned experience that is found within the pages of this book, we earnestly recommend that you read it from cover to cover. Later, when you want to review the operating details of a specific business, our simple alphabetical arrangement of the 100 businesses will enable you to zero in on your wealth opportunity instantly.

The Magic Formula for Success. These spare-time businesses provide you with the vital three C's of success—Capital, Credit and Confidence. This simple formula—C + C + C = Wealth—underlies all successful businesses, and each element is covered in this book. Here's how it works for you:

- CAPITAL—Success in any of the businesses described will give you a Wealth Base. Gold-seekers in old California called it a "grub-stake." As a modern wealth-seeker, you will use it the same way—as a start toward the discovery and accumulation of even greater wealth.

- CREDIT—When you invest your Wealth Base in an even bigger business you will find it remarkably easy to get someone else—a private backer or even a hard-nosed banker—to put vast sums of money into your venture. This pyramiding of capital gives you the leverage you need to grow in a chain reaction of wealth-producing successes. We show you how.
- CONFIDENCE—Persons not used to success find it hard to believe that they can build and control huge sums of money in a business of their own. Today, there are people from all walks of life who are enjoying new-found wealth and riches because they used the methods revealed to you in this book. Among these success stories are people who now handle $100,000 a year as easily as they formerly handled their weekly paychecks.

Every day the newspapers tell of new millionaires. We look forward to reading your story in the near future.

John Stockwell
Herbert Holtje

Contents

2. A Treasury of Money-Making, Spare-Time Opportunities
(*Continued*)

2. A Treasury of Money-Making, Spare-Time Opportunities
(Continued)

2. A Treasury of Money-Making, Spare-Time Opportunities
   (*Continued*)

2. A Treasury of Money-Making, Spare-Time Opportunities (*Continued*)

1

The Simple Discovery
That Makes Your
Business Success
Certain

Every successful businessman has discovered the "success principle" one way or another. Some were fortunate and learned
about it early in their careers. Others had to spend long, frustrat-
ing years of failure before they learned the secret that makes a fortune from a business enterprise that grows beyond the wildest
dreams of its founder.

Right now we are going to tell you this secret, so you will never
waste a minute of your time or a dollar of your money chasing
down a business blind alley. The simplest way to make this point
absolutely clear is to tell you the following true story. . . .

Harold Grant was a freshman at a big state university some
years ago. It was the first time he was away from home and he was
terribly lonely. And, he wasn't alone in his feeling, either. There
were literally thousands of other freshmen feeling "blue" just like
himself. Harold thought about this and then got an idea that he
felt sure would banish this feeling in short order.

Through a friend in the Admissions Office he got a list of all the freshmen who had just entered, together with their parents' names and addresses. Harold started writing to these parents telling them how lonely it was to be a freshman in completely strange surroundings, and also how they could help their sons and daughters get over this feeling. For only $5, he would personally arrange to have a surprise cake sent to their son or daughter with a welcome message of cheer from home.

The parents responded with a flood of five-dollar bills. Soon his business grew to the point where he had to make arrangements with a wholesale bakery, and also hire several assistants to handle the administrative details.

Harold returned to school the next year driving his new Thunderbird. If his idea worked so well at his school, why wouldn't it work equally well at other schools, he reasoned. He immediately set about expanding his staff of assistants and soon had representatives on over 20 large campuses working for him.

When he graduated with honor marks, Harold was making in excess of $20,000 a year, while working less than one day a week. He sold this business to an associate under a contract whereby he received a percentage of the profits for a period of 10 years. When we last spoke to Harold, he had received his final check from his buyer. His proceeds from the sale, over the years, had netted him over $80,000.

What This Story Tells You.   This story is a classic demonstration of the business success secret you *must* know if you expect to build your own Wealth Base like Harold. It is this:

Find a human need, satisfy it, and you will become rich.

Remember this statement. We will remind you of it again and again. Harold discovered this secret and couldn't help but make a fortune. Kids away from home for the first time get lonely and *need* someone to remember. Parents know this, and *need* some way to express their love and concern for their children. Harold understood these needs himself and merely thought of a simple way to satisfy the needs of both parent and child.

What People Need.   Here is a good time to see how well you have learned this principle. Take a few minutes and see how many needs you can add to these lists:

People *need* to be—

- happy
- wealthy
- healthy
- popular

People *need* to have—

- nice possessions
- comfort
- security
- social prestige

People *need* to avoid—

- discomfort
- hard work
- offending people
- embarrassment

All of these are basic human needs common to all of us. Any business you decide to start will fail or prosper depending on how well you satisfy these and other needs.

How to Turn a Need into a Proven, Moneymaking Business. By now, you should have this basic "need" principle firmly in mind. To be successful, you don't have to discover another fad like the hoola hoop, or strike oil, or hope to become rich with a once-in-a-million stroke of good fortune. Becoming rich in a business of your own, quickly and easily, means finding a need and satisfying it for money.

In the pages that follow, you will find scores of businesses built on this principle. Even though you may not think a particular business would interest you, please read it completely and carefully. Each business carries a lesson in need and satisfaction, and the more thoroughly you learn that lesson now, the more successful you can hope to become in the future.

Instant Money Can Be Yours. Believe it or not, most every business described in this book can be started for $100 or less. Their earning potential, for someone who will take the time to learn how to serve a human need, is limitless. What's more, many of these businesses practically run themselves.

At this point, you should realistically ask yourself what you consider a good spare-time income to be . . . $100 . . . $200 . . . $500 or more each week? The businesses we talk about can earn you this and more. Furthermore, they can be the springboard to the accumulation of great wealth. Once you have built your Wealth Base, you will have no trouble borrowing additional money to enable you to pyramid your Wealth Base automatically into a truly large fortune, practically without effort.

We assume that anyone reading this book has a full-time job, or has some sort of income he wishes to supplement in the beginning. Most businesses require that you set some measure of what your time is worth. Only *you* can answer that question, but here is a good rule to follow:

> Never work for less than what you earn on an hourly basis. If you are a salaried employee, compute your rate as if you were paid that way. You should strive for $1\frac{1}{2}$ to 2 times your hourly rate as a fair rate for your work or service.

Use this rate for establishing charges whenever we say you should charge for your time plus materials. This will produce a good rate of return on your work and investment, and you will move rapidly toward attaining the Wealth Base you seek.

How to Zoom Your Income Effortlessly.   In the pages following, you will find businesses suited to a wide variety of talents and interests. There is something here for everyone, even if only a germ of an idea for a completely new business. But—you must read every business to get maximum benefit from this book.

The chances are quite good that you will take one or more of these wealth-studded ideas and combine them to produce a unique, need-satisfying business of your very own. Like Harold Grant, whose story we told you at the beginning, you must find a need and a way to satisfy it. When you do, your Wealth Base is guaranteed, and you'll be on your way to the Big money at long last!

Your quest for wealth starts now. . . .

2

A Treasury of Money-Making, Spare-Time Opportunities

ADDRESSING SERVICE

Mail Yourself a Profit Every Month

Your Opportunity for Profit. Keep a sharp eye on your mailbox for the next month or two and you'll find an opportunity for making easy money at home with little or no investment. This opportunity was discovered by Mrs. Robert Adams, a widow who found inflation constantly eating away at her modest fixed income.

Mrs. Adams' mailbox, like that of millions of other people, is filled with mail that comes regularly each month from local sources—bills, statements, advertisements, newsletters, and announcements from merchants, groups, and various associations. Someone has to address and mail these letters, and Mrs. Adams found a way to do it at a neat profit virtually automatically, while working pleasantly at home. She now earns about $400 a month.

Local merchants and organizations can seldom afford a machine addressing operation because their lists are small, or they only have need for it once a month or so. Even though it is expensive, hand addressing is the least costly way of doing the job available to them. But, if *you* have an addressing machine, you can keep it busy most of the month handling these small jobs.

What You Can Earn.   There are mailing houses that address millions of pieces of mail each month—they are really big, multi-million-dollar businesses. Many of them started no bigger than what we are suggesting to you. As a home business, you can make a nice profit on your time and investment. The simplest, non-electric addressing machine can address about 500 pieces an hour. This is a slow rate of production, and you can quickly jump this to 700 or 800 pieces an hour. Electric machines, while more expensive, are even faster.

Here's how you charge for the various services you provide:

1. You charge a fixed rate for each name you put on stencil for use in your machine. Prices for blank stencils vary by machine, but a good rule is to charge a nickel a name, plus the cost of the stencil.
2. You charge for running the stencils to address pieces of mail supplied by your clients. The going rate is $20 per 1000 names—or 2¢ a name. For less than a 100 names, charge a minimum rate of $2.
3. You charge your clients for any changes they make in their mailing lists—usually 10¢ a name plus the cost of a new stencil.

Let's say one of your customers is a retail furniture store. Each month they mail out 1000 announcements to their customers announcing monthly sales. At $20 a 1000 names, you've earned yourself that amount for a little over an hour's work. Putting these names on stencils earned you 5¢ profit on each name over the cost of the stencil, and their monthly changes and additions, which can easily amount to 50 or 100 names can add another $10 to your income.

This one account is worth $30 or more a month to you. When you add the local gas station, variety store, and so on, you can easily run a $5000 a year business working a few hours a week.

HOW TO BUILD YOUR WEALTH BASE

Here's What You Need. First of all, you will need an addressing machine and a typewriter. Your present typewriter is probably adequate. In fact, an older machine, one that you strike hard to cut the stencils, is probably to be preferred over a newer, lighter machine.

Addressing machines come in many models, makes, and prices. Used machines are available from dealers who have taken them in trade, and a good, used machine should cost you less than $100.

How to Get Started. Start right now by keeping a list of all the businesses, organizations, political parties, and other groups that send you mail. Many such organizations want to mail to everyone in a given area. You might consider building a complete mailing list of your town so you can rent it out for such purposes. Your one-time investment in making up the list will be repaid the first few times the list is used. Keep it up-to-date by working with your post office and local tax collector who keeps track of people moving in and out of town.

How to Promote. The best way to promote this business is by making personal calls on all your likely prospects. If you save mailing pieces and announcements from local firms, you can use this as a starting point to explain your service and how you can eliminate their addressing headaches . . . and save them money to boot.

Your Opportunity for Growth. Once you have a complete mailing list of your trading area, you can rent this list as often as once a week at the $20 a 1000 rate. Every business you add to your list of clients will bring additional money. The next most logical growth step is to add other business services. Some of them are explained in other parts of this book—for example: complete letter-shop services, bookkeeping services, and advertising distribution services.

ADVERTISING DISTRIBUTION SERVICES

Make Money by Giving Things Away

Your Opportunity for Profit.   Under most circumstances, local retail store operators have only two ways of attracting business:

- advertising in local newspapers
- direct mail to the people in their trading area

However, there is another very effective way of developing business—direct advertising distribution. That is, store owners get their message, or product samples distributed directly to the residents in their area. This can often be more expensive than either newspaper advertising or direct mail, unless you, an advertising distributor, can show prospects the secret of making it work economically.

Bernie Callahan stumbled onto the secret while looking for a way to augment his meager weekly salary as a retail store clerk. Part of his job was to distribute circulars in the immediate neighborhood announcing his store's weekly "specials." He figured that if he could distribute ads for one store, it would be just as easy to drop two, three, or more non-competing advertisements when making the rounds. And so was born the idea of the cooperative advertising distribution business.

Of course, Bernie found it impossible to cover the town himself, so he soon recruited helpers who were looking for part-time income. Soon, Bernie was independent as the owner of a growing business, making hundreds of dollars a week.

What You Can Earn.   Start with the minimum wage that you can pay to people for the actual work of distribution, and then figure how many "drops" they can make per hour. Let's say you pay your workers $1.50 an hour, as Bernie did, and they average 40 drops in an hour. This means that each drop is costing you about 4¢.

You should triple this figure to make money on the deal. In this example, the total charge per house drop comes to 12¢. If you have four merchants participating in this cooperative drop, the charge to each works out to one-quarter of that amount, or 3¢. This is a very inexpensive way of getting a message in a person's home—for less than direct mail. Your profit per drop is 8¢, or $3.20 per hour. And you don't have to leave your office to earn this.

In a small town, like that in which Bernie Callahan started his business, you can have at least 10 people working 8 hours on a Saturday to cover all residents and come up with a profit on 80 man hours of work, or $256. If you keep it to Saturdays, and one area, it is possible to make at least $12,000 a year, as did Bernie, for simply lining up the work and the workers. Bernie's secret lies in the fact that he drops many pieces at each home in his cooperative distribution service.

HOW TO BUILD YOUR WEALTH BASE

Here's What You Need.   In a word, you need people. Recruit them from among your friends, fellow lodge members, or thru classified ads in the newspaper.

How to Get Started.   Contact *all* the merchants in town, and tell them of your cooperative direct advertising system. Be sure to show them that your cost per contact is less than what they would pay to reach the same number of people with direct mail or newspaper ads. To get the ammunition you need, get a current advertising rate card from the newspaper, and compute the cost to reach the audience with an ad. You will always come out on top.

How to Promote.   This business is best promoted by direct contact. After all, it is a direct contact service which you are selling. When you talk to the merchants emphasize these points:

- direct advertising is just that—direct and active
- you can control the time of exposure for special sales
- it is much more personal
- it is much more effective than any other way of retail promotion
- the cost is less than any other method—because of it being a cooperative venture with other merchants

Many retailers may at first be at a loss to have anything to distribute. Be quick to point out that their suppliers will often give them, at no charge, sales literature imprinted with their name.
Your Opportunity for Growth.   If you've covered your town, move on. Recruit teams in nearby towns to do the same thing.

A word of caution: The home mailbox, even though owned by the householder is sacred—do not put any of your material in it. Federal law prohibits its use for anything but government stamped mail. Use the newspaper rack, slide it under the door, hook it to the knob, or provide an inexpensive plastic bag, with a loop for the knob—at an extra charge, of course.

AIR CONDITIONER
INSTALLATION SERVICE

Cool Cash for You

Your Opportunity for Profit.   Most homeowners with room-type air conditioners remove them for the winter to prevent ice damage. At best, it is a burdensome job for the homeowner. If it is done by an air conditioner, or electrical service company, the homeowner can pay as much as $20 per removal, and the same amount to re-install in the spring.

In this business, which is easily expandable to a complete air conditioner service, the operator contacts everyone in his area with room air conditioners, and establishes a "route" of spring installations and fall removals. He can also include filter cleaning and minor mounting adjustments.

What You Can Earn. Because you will be operating a "one-service" business at the start, and because you can do—efficiently, and economically what the larger contractors cannot, and usually do not want to do, you can afford to charge less. Obviously, at a lower price, it is possible to increase volume, and corresponding sales.

Joe Polachek runs this service and charges $12 to $15 per installation or removal, and a flat price of $25 if the homeowner agrees to a yearly contract. With 40 customers the first year he started, Joe was $1,000 richer without too much work. Almost overnight, he had started a fortune-making business.

HOW TO BUILD YOUR WEALTH BASE

Here's What You Need. Physically, you should be in reasonably good shape. An assistant would help for the big ones, but you should be able to get an after-school boy to help for relatively low cost. You will need no equipment, other than several size screwdrivers, a pair of pliers, and a set of adjustable wrenches.

How to Get Started. Cruise your own neighborhood to start. Note the address of every house with an air conditioner in the window. Next try the same thing with other sections of your town, and nearby towns. Look to identify areas with a heavy concentration of such installations. This is where you start. After all, the shorter the distance from job to job, the more time you'll have to work, and get paid.

How to Promote. After you have identified the areas where you can find the most air conditioners, prepare a simple post card mailer—even a hand-written announcement will do, and mail it to the addresses you have recorded from your travels. Tell them what you are doing, how much it will cost, and above all—what they will save, both in terms of time and sore muscles if they do it themselves, and money if they have a contractor doing it. Next, follow up those who did not respond to your mailing with a personal call. Call in the early evening to catch the man of the house, who usually has to do the job.

Your Opportunity for Growth.   Once you have established yourself as a reliable craftsman, it is only a short step to the service of testing air conditioners for Freon level, and recharging them where necessary. This involves only a small investment in a gauge and Freon tank, usually less than $75. During the initial establishment of the business, it would be wise for the proprietor to begin taking a course in air conditioning servicing in order to expand the scope of the business, and, of course, the profits. Courses are available as correspondence home study, or often thru your local trade or vocational high school.

ANTIQUE REBUILDING
AND REFINISHING

Priceless Possessions Mean Profits for You

Your Opportunity for Profit.   Interest in antiques never seems to wane. If anything, *interest and prices* keep on rising year after year. This growing market can provide you with a dependable source of income, good times and bad. Making this business pay requires a liking for working with your hands, but you don't need the skill and experience of an expert cabinetmaker. Most real antiques were handmade, in home workshops, with relatively simple hand tools.

You earn money in a variety of ways. For example:

1. *Antique refinishing.* Usually, someone has found an old piece in a barn or at an auction, and wants years of paint removed and the natural finish restored.

2. *Antique rebuilding or repair.* First-class pieces are scarce. Most buyers have to content themselves with items that are lacking in parts, or need some repair to make them serviceable.

3. *Antique faking.* Yes, faking. Buyers often can't buy a piece that fits all their specifications as regards design, period, color and size. For them, you buy a new or unfinished piece and try to duplicate some of the age of a real antique.

A few simple tricks, plus a few hand tools, can put you in this business quickly and easily. You can have a backlog of interesting, profitable work in no time at all.

What You Can Earn. You'll probably work at less than your true worth in the beginning. Until you gain experience, you will probably estimate your time too low. Basically, this is a business where you charge for the hours you work. Don't be afraid to charge $5 to $10 per hour for your time. Remember—people are very careful to whom they entrust heirlooms and other valuable items. Ten hours a week of relaxing work in your workshop (which you probably do free right now) can bring you $50 to $100 a week in welcome income.

HOW TO BUILD YOUR WEALTH BASE

Here's What You Need. The tools you will need, even if you want to go deeply into this business, should not cost you too much. You will need basic items like hammers, saws, scrapers, drills, and rasps. An electric drill that can be adapted for buffing or sanding is a good investment, even though it was unknown at the time the piece was made.

If you expect to do restoration work, a power saw and a woodworking lathe will be necessary. For faking antiques, provide yourself with a variety of roughing tools to round edges and duplicate worn spots. One of the best "tools" for improvising the nicks and scratches of age is a few feet of heavy chain. You literally "beat" the pieces with the chain to make marks suggesting age, and the effect is more realistic than the hammer marks often passed off as "distressing" in commercial pieces.

How to Get Started.   Get to know all the antique dealers in the neighborhood. Show them samples of your work, and before you know it, they will give you all the work you can handle. If you work for a dealer, you should consider some sort of "wholesale" rate because you won't have any promotion expenses to get the business.

How to Promote.   Another way to attract customers is to run small, regular ads in the classified pages of your newspaper and in the yellow pages of the telephone directory. If there is an antique fair nearby, consider taking a booth and putting on a demonstration of antique refinishing. Finally, because courses in this subject are so popular, you might consider offering lessons at the local adult school. True, you might lose some business to people who will decide to do their own work. But this is offset usually by the increase in your reputation, and the prices you can charge in the future.

Your Opportunity for Growth.   This is a business that can be kept in your home workshop for as long as you like. On the other hand, it can be lucrative enough to open a regular shop later on and to add helpers to do the work under your supervision.

   You should also consider adding chair caning, stenciling and decorating, and other business as adjuncts to this operation.

ART BROKER

The "Art" of Making Money

Your Opportunity for Profit.   Here's a familiar situation: you're among a group of friends and the conversation turns to art. You feel out of place because some of your friends can draw, paint, or turn a lump of clay into someone you can recognize instantly. All you can do is say, "I wish I had talent."

Wish no more! Take a leaf from the page of Helen Kent who found herself in just such a spot. When she discovered one simple secret, she immediately became the most popular and sought after person among that group of "arty" friends. She became an art broker and enjoyed the following:

1. she was the most important one in this little group—she actually sold the others' artistic creations!
2. she earned commissions on every sale
3. and she had a constantly changing art exhibit in her own home.

What You Can Earn. This is a delightful way to add to your Wealth Base, with this one added advantage—there is always a chance that one of your friends will become fairly well known and sought after. If that happens, you've tied yourself to a star that can bring you fortune. Helen Kent never was *that* lucky, but she did manage to earn $5800 working part time during the year.

HOW TO BUILD YOUR WEALTH BASE

Here's What You Need. Basically, all you need is a group of people with some talent in the arts. If you don't know too many of them, you can find them by joining clubs or classes in town, by going to lectures, or even advertising for them. Put a little ad in the paper that says an "art dealer wishes to add one or two more talented painters to the group of artists he represents" and your phone will be busy for a week. Your biggest job will be to judge, with some accuracy, those artists who can paint salable pictures.
How to Get Started. Line up a group of artists who will agree to work through you whenever any of their works may be sold. This is important. You don't want to develop a market for a certain person's work and then discover that he is selling things himself and eliminating your just commissions.

Have the artists sign a simple agreement—similar to what you would sign if you gave a real-estate agent an exclusive offering to sell your house. You should get at least one third of the selling price as your commission.

Get several of your artists' works for display and live with them in your own home for a while. It's amazing how some things will grow on you, and how others will quickly pall. This is a good indication of which items will be most easily sold. Also, check your insurance coverage. Usually, the artist is responsible for insuring his own work.

How to Promote.   Most of your promotions won't cost you anything. Rather, you should become skilled in public relations and get as much free publicity as possible. You can do it in various ways:

1. Offer to put on free "art shows" at your local library, service club, school, or church group.
2. Develop a "story" about your artists and try to get some stories in your local paper about one of them from time to time.
3. Work with decorators, designers, architects, and buyers in department or furniture stores. Many times you can work a "consignment" deal with them.

And, of course, your biggest promotion is the permanent display you have in your own home. Don't be afraid to show everyone who comes to visit you some recent additions to your collection.

Your Opportunity for Growth.   Your growth will come in two ways: you will add more and more artists to your string; and you will be able to increase prices of certain works as the artists gain a certain reputation and following. Minor fads can develop rather quickly. A customer buys a seascape by a certain artist through you. Her friends see the picture, and soon they all come to you wanting similar seascapes by the same artist. Be ready to capitalize on situations such as this.

ARTS AND CRAFTS EXCHANGE

Profit from the Talent of Others

Your Opportunity for Profit.   Nellie Karp had an aunt who could make scarves at a rate that was nothing short of being amazing. Her uncle was a whiz at producing craft projects in his basement workshop. Once the neighbors and relatives had been given craft gifts to the limit, there was little else they could do except to pile up scarves and birdhouses.

A neighbor who was not quite as talented as the pair, but who recognized the value of their hobby, suggested that they try to sell some of the things they made. Neither knew how to go about it, and asked the neighbor if he would give them a hand.

Friend neighbor came up with an Arts and Crafts Exchange—a business which costs nothing to start, but can net thousands of dollars a year. He simply set up some borrowed card tables, and began to display the work of his friends. His profits were based strictly on what he sold in his consignment shop.

What You Can Earn.   Because this is a consignment business in which you make money only when you make a sale, it is impossible to predict what you can actually make. However, most similar operations work on a mark-up of 40% of the hobbyist's price. If the hobbyist wants $10 for an item, you add 40% or $4 to his price to get your selling price, $14.00. Because your initial overhead will be zero, this figure represents a substantial profit for a few spare-time hours of very pleasant work.

HOW TO BUILD YOUR WEALTH BASE

Here's What You Need.   You must be able to spot good work in a variety of areas—sewing, woodworking, art, ceramics, etc. Many people who have made a success of this type of business began with specific knowledge in one area—woodworking, for example —and developed an understanding of other products later on.

You will need a place to display your consigned wares. If you use your home or garage, you'd better check the local zoning ordinances. Otherwise, you might consider renting a small store off the main business street where rents are often considerably lower.

How to Get Started.   First, find out what salable talent exists in your neighborhood and family. Be careful! Everybody with a hobby is quite proud of their ability, and are seldom as critical as a customer.

When you have lined up the talent you need, try to get each of them to produce some samples for you. If you've rented a store, fill out the store as much as possible.

How to Promote.   To get started, you might consider exhibiting at local fairs and craft shows, and at fund raising affairs of churches and other groups. Here's where you use the samples your suppliers have produced. Try running ads in the classified section of your local newspaper. Placing an ad under "personals" can often be more effective than placing one in the "articles for sale" section.

Your Opportunity for Growth.   This business is perfect for the person who wants to get into direct mail. Once your sources of supply are established, and you know that you can count on them, begin making mailings.

An invaluable treasury of mail-order success techniques is sent free to every subscriber to *The Franklin Letter*. This is a monthly newsletter read by wealth-seeking individuals looking for solid information on business opportunities. A year's subscription costs $18 and is available by sending a check to James Franklin Associates, Box 95, Demarest, New Jersey 07627.

ATTIC AND CELLAR CLEANING

Find Money in Other People's Attics

Your Opportunity for Profit.   With a small truck and a strong back, you can get into the business of cleaning cellars and attics of accumulated trash and junk. Most men who have gone into this business have never let their ambitions run beyond this. However, if you use your head, as well as your back, the opportunity for making money is increased to an incredible extent.

America's attics and cellars are teeming with junk. Yet, one man's junk is another man's "treasure." If you doubt this, go to a "white-elephant" sale or rummage sale, and see what people will pay for "junk."

Most of the junk you collect will be disposed of at the town dump. But, you get a crack at some potentially valuable items that can make the hours of work profitable to a degree you may never have thought possible. If you have a shred of gambling instinct in you, you'll love this business, because you'll never know in advance when you strike a really valuable find.

What You Can Earn. Usually payment is by the hour for the use of your back and a truck. Your time, plus that of a husky teenager and truck, is easily worth $8 to $12 an hour. Implicit in your agreement with the owner of the junk is that you get to keep it when you drive off to the dump.

What valuable items can you find that will make this job worthwhile? An original Lincoln letter? Very unlikely. Instead, you're more likely to find bundles of old magazines, dirty bottles and jars, and other nondescript odds and ends.

But . . . did you know that:

- some movie fan magazines and comic books of the 30's and 40's command prices as high as $300 from avid collectors?
- old sheet music (that some people saved by the trunk load) is now being framed and sold as decorative pictures by smart shops for $25 or more?
- or that old medicine bottles are eagerly sought after, and certain old-fashioned Mason jars sell for $3 apiece in antique shops.

These few examples should suggest that items no more than thirty years old are now valuable collector's items.

HOW TO BUILD YOUR WEALTH BASE

Here's What You Need. A willingness to work, a small truck, owned or leased for the job, plus a pair of sharp eyes are all you need to get started.

How to Get Started. Seek out some knowledgeable antique dealer and tell him what you propose to do. If you promise him first crack at items you find, in return he should give you a short course in what to look for. This will do two things for you:

- you will know some of the collectable items that are currently selling, whether they are items representing nostalgia (like old magazines or comic books) or actual antiques
- you will have a ready market for your finds without having to get too deeply involved in selling

How to Promote. Small ads are a necessity. Usually, newspapers have a heading called "hauling" that you can use. Consistency will pay off here. You will find that people turn to these ads for this and similar services.

Another effective device is to cruise the older sections of town. *Not* the run-down sections, but rather areas of older, more substantial homes. Here are people with the money needed to engage your services, and with attics that probably are bulging with accumulations of junk from several decades.

Get the addresses of likely looking prospects and drop each occupant a simple postcard describing your reasonably priced attic and cellar hauling service.

Your Opportunity for Growth. As a simple hauling business, you can make money only by the number of jobs you are able to take. At $10 an hour or so, this is a hard, but well-paying way to build a Wealth Base. However, if you work diligently at learning what to look for, the amount of money you can earn is really impossible to predict.

"Now, at $25 a copy, what would this old trunk full of movie fan magazines be worth?" Someday you might be muttering this question to yourself in a corner of somebody's attic. Even if you're not this lucky, chances are you can find enough interesting objects that can be turned into lamps as described in the section on "Custom Lamp Making."

AUDIO-VISUAL SERVICES

Project Your Way to Profits

Your Opportunity for Profit.   If you've ever gone to a meeting at a school, church, business organization, town body, or whatever, you've been exposed to audio-visual aids of one sort or another.

You watched a dim movie, dozed through fuzzy slides, and squinted at hard-to-read charts and signs. Even the explanations that go with these presentations seem to break down. Seldom do you come across a good public address system, one that is adjusted for the room in which it is being used, and placed so that everyone can hear comfortably.

The point is simply this—with a little easily-acquired professional knowledge you can offer a worthwhile and highly sought-after service. You can become the audio-visual expert who makes a dull meeting come to life. You can offer organizations and businesses a service that will help them

- show slides and movies at their best—the right size screen, the right brightness, and the right viewing conditions for each particular audience
- adjust public address systems to eliminate all the squeals and noises that come from faulty settings, poorly placed speakers, and awkwardly located microphones
- create charts and graphs that show needed information so that viewers will get the information they were intended to get—without squinting, or being confused with meaningless details
- and a host of other jobs to make the whole business of communicating with a group easier for the organization using your services.

In short, you become the professional that others turn to whenever they have a need to put on a meeting requiring well-handled sight and sound.

What You Can Earn.   Most meetings in town seem to take place at night—which makes it ideal for you if you happen to hold down a full-time daytime job. If you provide service only, then the most you can earn will be an hourly rate for the time you actually spend on the job. In many cases, this hourly rate can be much more than what you earn at your regular job. It is not unusual to charge $15 to $25 for a few hours work in an evening.

HOW TO BUILD YOUR WEALTH BASE

Here's What You Need.   You'll need some background knowledge in working various types of projectors and public address systems. Each projector is different in detail, but the basic operation is the same for all similar types. After you've worked with a few different types, you'll quickly get the hang of operation and will be able to take a strange machine and make it work right the first time you handle it.

How to Get Started.   Call on the various prospects in town. These include businessmen, usually with salespersons on their staff or with a number of trainees; charitable and fraternal organizations that put on programs for themselves or larger groups; and just about any other organization engaged in some sort of educational program.

How to Promote.   Another source of leads is the banquet manager of the hotel in town. Many groups will hold a meeting at a hotel, or motel, and plan to put on a program involving audio-visual aids of one sort or another. Most hotels do not have anyone on their staff for this and simply refer such requests to outside individuals.

Your Opportunity for Growth.   Working by yourself will limit your income to the number of hours you can spend. You can add to your income by getting into the production of visual aids and offering that as part of your service. Sign making is another service that is easily worked into your overall operation.

AUTO DIAGNOSIS

This Can Drive Up Your Profits

Your Opportunity for Profit. Most gas stations are good at one thing—selling gas. Ask them to do more than a minor repair, and they are in trouble—and so are you. But, given a proper diagnosis of the trouble, and even the least knowledgeable of service station attendants can often do the job.

When a car simply stops dead, there are many things that can be wrong. The same is true of loss of power, and all the other things that can go wrong with it. The poor mechanic will spend time on irrelevant things until he stumbles on the problem. But, equipped with a basic knowledge of auto operation, and a set of inexpensive tools and instruments, the "Auto-Diagnostician" can put his finger on the trouble in minutes. He does not waste time on parts that he knows would not cause the problem.

Once the trouble is spotted, the owner can fix it, he can have a conventional service station do the work, or the diagnostician himself may sometimes do the work. Anyway it's handled, you can make money in this field.

What You Can Earn. If you do strictly diagnostic work, you must charge either a flat fee, or an hourly rate. The flat fee is best, because, as a skilled technician, you can often spot the trouble in minutes. And, after all, it is the "answer" you are selling, not the time it takes to find the problem. And because this service is more valuable as a diagnosis of "healthy" cars to keep them running, rather than that of getting the stalled ones back on the road, you can charge at least $25 for a complete report on the car's "health." You should limit yourself to engine, ignition, brake, and power train analysis. Stay away from body and wheel alignment. The competition is keen and the equipment is costly.

HOW TO BUILD YOUR WEALTH BASE

Here's What You Need.   For about $100 you can buy a set of test instruments that, coupled with your skill, will allow you to diagnose a car's state of health quickly and effectively. Sears, Montgomery Ward, Whitney, and even the local auto parts shops carry these instruments. You should start off with: a dwell tachometer, alternator tester, ignition tester, compression gauge, vacuum gauge, timing light, and an exhaust analyzer. A set of simple tools—pliers, wrenches, screw drivers, hammer, and feeler gauges—should be included.

How to Get Started.   Look for a few gas stations, near large factories, which specialize in a high volume of gas sales, and have little technical competence. Tell them of your service, and ask them to tell their customers, many of whom work at the nearby plants. Explain, that if their customers leave their cars for the day at the station while they are at work and do not need the car, you will perform the diagnosis for a small fee. Your friend, the station owner, then gets to do the repairs, and you both profit.

How to Promote.   If you don't get enough business by the way we just described, you could supplement the effort by local advertising in both the phone book yellow pages, and the classified pages of the newspaper in town. You might also send out mailings to a resident list, often available from local mailing houses.

Your Opportunity for Growth.   This is the kind of business that, once it gets going, would provide you with more work than you ever dreamed of. The dissatisfaction with most so-called mechanics runs high, and a top-flight diagnostic service is a much needed business.

To grow, your best bet is to simply add skilled diagnosticians, like yourself, rather than get involved with the actual dirty work of doing the repairs. You might add a complete tune-up service, but pass on the motor jobs to someone equipped for the work.

AUTO PICK UP AND DELIVERY

Your Driver's License Is Worth Money

Your Opportunity for Profit. Most of the time, people take their cars for granted. No piece of machinery has ever been invented that is so complicated, and yet demands so little from the owner in knowledge or care. When the car does need service, the owner usually finds the job of delivering and picking up his car the most inconvenient part of ownership.

Some gas stations provide pick-up and delivery service for their customers. You can be that person and pick up extra money. New car dealers usually get only part of the service business they would get *if* the new car owner remembered to bring his car in at the recommended mileages. You can remind the customer and deliver the car to the dealer for regular service.

Some states require cars to be run through an inspection station—a job that most car owners dread because it uses up part of a day. You can do this job, at a price, for the owner. A businessman goes away on a business trip. You can drive his car to the airport when he is expected to return; you'll earn money for the trip, and the businessman will still save money because he avoided long term parking fees and potential damage to his car in the airport parking lot.

You can think up ways of using your license to earn money driving other people's cars. If you add the money you can make driving your own car (like the private transportation business mentioned elsewhere) then you've got a solid part-time business.

What You Can Earn. All you can charge for in this business is your time. You have, by now, put some value on your spare hours, and you should charge accordingly. Keep in mind one fact— charge for *all* your hours. Keep track of the time you may spend waiting.

Your hourly rate, multiplied by the hours of work you can manage in your free time, equals *total* profit. There are no expenses or materials to be paid for.

HOW TO BUILD YOUR WEALTH BASE

Here's What You Need.   First, of course, is a driver's license. Other than that, nothing else is required, except a reputation for carefulness and reliability. People like to know that anyone driving their car will be just as careful as they would be.

You had better check with your insurance man to see if any extra coverage should be acquired. A person driving a car for someone else can run up quite a liability if he should become involved in an accident.

How to Get Started.   There is nothing like a "uniform" to impress people with your reliability and concern. Look at your milkman or some other delivery man that calls at your home. Chances are he has some kind of uniform. Get yourself a neat jacket and cap from a uniform supply house before you start your rounds.

How to Promote.   The best way to promote is to call on the local car dealers and gas stations and tell them what you have in mind. Even if they can't use you at the moment, they can usually tell you of some customer who is looking for help.

Your Opportunity for Growth.   Growth is possible only by adding more hours to your working day. If you want to add a helper, be sure he is just as reliable as yourself.

BABY SITTING COORDINATOR

The Watched Tot Brings Profits

Your Opportunity for Profit.   If you're a parent, consider the number of times you've had to cancel a date, or miss a good movie just because there wasn't a baby sitter available. Why not turn this situation into a source of sitters, and profit?

The idea here is to set up a central clearing house, a large list of everybody within several miles who is willing to baby sit, for how much, and when they are available. Then you advertise the service and place the sitters as needed and collect the profits.

What You Can Earn.   The best way to make money here is to establish a flat rate, which each of your sitters charge, and then have them give you a percentage of their income from jobs referred by you. The going rate varies from one part of the country to another, but in the eastern suburbs, for example, the going rate is about $1 an hour, with an added 50¢ after the clock strikes midnight.

For the service of locating the jobs, you can charge the sitters 20% to 25% of their income. But, and be careful here; some states have rigid regulations governing this business. Some states actually class this business as sort of an employment agency, and set the rates and require a detailed registration. In other states, as long as you do not bill the parents, there is no problem. Be sure to check this out with your State Department of Labor before you begin. A phone call to their local office is sufficient.

HOW TO BUILD YOUR WEALTH BASE

Here's What You Need.   Basically, all you will need is a telephone, preferably a line separate from your private line if you operate this business from your home, and some method of keeping careful records. Usually 3 x 5 file cards and a file tray will suffice.

How to Get Started.   You have to get to two groups here—the sitters, and the parents seeking sitters. To get the sitters, first spread the word to your friends with high-school girls who might be interested. Ask the women's clubs to recommend any senior members who might like to earn extra money, and be sure to post notices on church, school and club bulletin boards.

How to Promote.   Once you have a fair number of sitters, you can begin talking up the service. Run ads in the classified pages of your local paper, and be sure to have announcements made at PTA meetings.

Your Opportunity for Growth.   The only way to grow is to add to your list of sitters and parents in need of them. Obviously, you can handle quite a number of each before it becomes too much for one person. You might consider "franchising" this business to someone in another location. You supply the know-how to start him for a flat fee, and then collect a percentage of his annual income. The employment agency franchise deals work quite successfully this way.

BOOKBINDING SERVICE

Old Books Make Your Bankbook Grow

Your Opportunity for Profit.   Even the smallest library or school has several thousand books within its walls—books that are constantly being used, abused, and worn out. Usually, the covers and binding of the books take the worst beating. Pages seldom wear out. For this reason, it is economical for a library to regularly rebind worn-out books rather than spend the money replacing them. This is where you can help, and earn yourself a stable and secure part-time income.

Large libraries often do the work themselves, but smaller libraries, particularly in smaller towns and cities, usually send the work out to companies that solicit their work by mail. Most librarians, however, would rather deal with a reliable, local person because they could

- enjoy faster, more personalized service
- eliminate the bother of wrapping and mailing books
- avoid the prospect of losing a book that is valuable and no longer in print.

Your job is simplicity itself. You pick up worn books at the school or library, take them home for working at your leisure, and then return them—with a bill. The work is easily learned, pleasant, and requires no elaborate equipment.

What You Can Earn.   If you want to earn a modest sideline income, the $2 to $3 per volume you collect will be a pleasant reward for your labors. However, the business can be expanded without too much trouble, by adding helpers to your staff.

After you've gotten some experience yourself, it should be easy to pass your knowledge on to others—your wife, friends, and even others in town looking for ways to augment their income.

If you charge $3 per volume, you can pay your helpers $2 per book. The remaining $1 is payment for your work in getting and servicing the various accounts you have built up.

HOW TO BUILD YOUR WEALTH BASE

Here's What You Need.   You'll need some simple bookbinding tools; such as glue pot and brush, sewing awl, trimming knife, and a simple press. Depending on how elaborate you wish to get, the whole set should run between $15 and $50. Big mail-order houses and hobby dealers usually carry bookbinding kits. Check their catalogs, and compare prices before you buy.

How to Get Started.   Call your local librarian to see what potential exists right at your doorstep. She can direct you to librarians in adjoining towns so you can figure out your potential earnings. Once you've decided to go ahead and invest in the bookbinding materials, practice on a few old books of your own. In short order you will be ready to call on accounts, offering a much needed, local bookbinding service.

How to Promote.   In the beginning, the simplest way to get business is to call on the librarian during the hours when she's not too busy. That way, she will have the time to talk to you at length. Take along one or two samples to demonstrate the kind of work you do. Since bookbinding costs are usually part of every library budget, to be spent at the discretion of the librarian, you can walk away with several orders immediately.

Your Opportunity for Growth.   Bookbinding is a one-by-one operation—there is no way of mass-producing the work other than adding more hands to the job. This you can easily do, because the work is attractive to a lot of people who like to work at home. Large companies, particularly engineering firms, bind their papers and drawings. Don't overlook this as a good source of income.

BUILDERS' CLEAN-UP SERVICE

Be a No-Overhead Contractor

Your Opportunity for Profit.   When a builder or general contractor builds a home, commercial building, or store, he deals with a number of major sub-contractors—masons, carpenters, plumbers, electricians, and so on. When they are all finished with their jobs, the building still isn't finished. It must be put in "broom-clean" condition before it is turned over to the new owner.

What this involves is more than sweeping. A hundred-and-one little clean-up jobs must be done and none of the major contractors is really responsible for doing them. This is where you can offer a needed and valuable service, and, in effect, become a regular sub-contractor yourself.

For example, here are some of the jobs that must be done in a new building to make it "broom-clean" . . .

- layers of paper used for protection in shipping must be peeled off bathtubs and plumbing fixtures
- windows must be scraped to get rid of the paint and labels on all panels of glass
- debris of all sort inside and outside the house must be picked up and placed where it can be removed by a scavenger
- doors must be placed on their proper hinges all over the house (good painters remove them before painting)
- electrical fixtures need light bulbs and glass parts installed
- and so on . . .

What You Can Earn. There are two ways you can charge for this service—by the hour or by the job. An hourly rate with an estimate given in writing before you start is best if you're starting an unfamiliar job, or if both you and the builder feel that the number of hours needed is uncertain.

A "job-rate" can be charged when most of the projects are similar—as for example, when the builder is putting up a group of similar homes in one area and the same jobs need to be done in each of the houses. A charge of $50 to $100 per house is reasonable, and represents less than two days work on your part. This work can also be done in the evening, when the other major contractors have left and when you have the spare time available.

HOW TO BUILD YOUR WEALTH BASE

Here's What You Need. You will require little, if anything, in the way of tools or equipment. Look over the job before taking it and you will see what is needed in the way of scrapers, brooms, or a few simple tools like screwdrivers and pliers. Some old rags and cleaning supplies complete your tool kit.

How to Get Started. Read the chapter on advertising to understand the essentials of a good sales letter. Then write a letter to half a dozen or so contractors or builders in your area. Talk to the man at the local lumber yard and ask him to recommend your service to the builders who are his customers. And, of course, the simplest approach is to drive around where a development is going up, seek out the builder or foreman, and tell him directly of the service you have to offer.

How to Promote.   In selling the plan to builders, be sure to point out the positive benefits that will accrue through the use of your "broom-clean" service. Most homeowners will keep calling the builder with a hundred-and-one small complaints after they move in. By minimizing the complaints, the builder . . .

- gets a reputation for building houses that satisfy their own- ers
- spends less time on unproductive "call-backs" to the job and can concentrate on the money-making new jobs

Your Opportunity for Growth.   Your growth here is limited by your time or the size of the business you want to build up. Obviously, as you get busy, you can add people to your staff and let them do the clean-up work while you do the selling. It should be easy to find workers, because every town has an available supply of young men or older workers looking for a few extra hours work a week. You charge for their labor, plus a profit for yourself in estimating and supervising the job.

CAMP EQUIPMENT EXCHANGE

Getting Rich by Someone Else's Fireside

Your Opportunity for Profit.   With America becoming a nation of family campers, you have the opportunity to profit from a needed service business. We mentioned in other parts of this book various businesses built on exchanging and loaning equipment.

Running a camp equipment exchange can be particularly rewarding because there are so many prospects for this service, and also, so many sources of equipment to loan.

For example: The Jones family spent quite a bit of money on a tent for their vacation trips. They use the tent two weeks in June. The rest of the year it is stored in their attic. The Smith family would like to go camping for two weeks in August. Rather than spend the money on a tent of their own, they would be willing to spend $30 or $40 to rent one. Now . . . if only someone could introduce the Smith family to the Jones family. This is where you come in, with your year-round camp equipment exchange.

In a nutshell: you get as many people as possible to join your camp equipment exchange. Two things are essential for membership—a nominal membership fee (which pays all your expenses) and some equipment they are willing to rent. You list the equipment in your equipment exchange. When the Smith family rents their tent to the Jones' through your service, you charge the Smiths a commission for finding a renter.

What You Can Earn.   This business is best started on an area basis. You will have to be close enough to pick up and deliver equipment without spending all your time on the road. In a 30 mile radius from your home, you should normally find enough of prospects to support quite a lucrative part-time business.

Each member pays $5 for an annual membership. This permits him to list his equipment in your equipment exchange for the whole season. When he rents his listed equipment, you get 20% of the rental fee. Rental fees will vary with the type of equipment, obviously. A pair of camp cots will rent for less than a large wall tent. A rough rule of thumb for setting rental fees is to charge 10% to 15% of the value of the equipment for two weeks use. A tent worth $300 is worth $30 to $45 when rented to a family, and earns you $6 to $9 in commissions.

Each member gets a simple mimeographed "newsletter" from you in which you list the equipment for rent and the times it will be available. This letter can go out once a month during the vacation season, and perhaps twice during the fall and winter months. All the items for rent are identified by a code number, so the would-be renters have to work through you to protect your commission.

You can increase the value of this equipment newsletter to your members by including some camping hints or hints from other members. One of your members may have found some out-of-the way-spot they would like to recommend to others, or some hint to make camp life easier, or what have you.

With 100 members, you immediately earn $500 from membership fees. With 100 members, it's not unlikely that you can earn another $1000 commissions on rental fees. With 1000 members (which this business can easily grow to) you can increase these figures ten times.

HOW TO BUILD YOUR WEALTH BASE

Here's What You Need.   You don't even have to own a camp stool to start this business. Neither do you have to be a camper yourself. It would help though if you knew something about camping so you know what equipment is most useful, and therefore, most rentable.

How to Get Started.   Do some basic market research in your area to determine how many camping families there are that you can service. You'll probably be surprised at the number on your own block alone. Check, too, how many new equipment dealers there are in the area. This will give you an idea of the potential in your locality.

Start talking up your business, and before you know it, you'll have quite a list of people willing to rent their idle equipment. These can be your "charter members" of the camping club, and be listed in your first issue of the newsletter. You've got to have a sample of the letter to be able to promote the service.

How to Promote.   The ideal way to promote this service is to interest the editor of your local paper in running a story on your unique business as a feature article. This will get you loads of inquiries. Lacking such a piece of luck, try small ads in his paper in the classified column because people usually turn to these pages when they want to rent something. Once your newsletter is running, you have an ideal tool to promote new memberships. Simply offer each member some incentive to get another member for you —an "every member get one" campaign. Your incentive can be a reduced rate for the person getting you another member, or better yet, some low-cost, but needed camp item that everyone can use. **Your Opportunity for Growth.** Growth comes from increasing the number of members, and this can be almost limitless. When the members become widespread, add assistants in other locations to handle the delivery details so you don't have to travel. In fact, when that time comes, you'll probably have your own assistants, while you'll be concentrating on turning out an eagerly looked for camp "newsletter" to your subscribers each month.

CAR POOL COORDINATOR

Cash from Commuters

Your Opportunity for Profit. The car pool is a popular way to get to work in every metropolitan area. However, most car pools are loosely organized groups of neighbors who happen to work near each other in the city. They get together almost by accident, but a smart businessman can cash in on this money-saving way to get to work by actually organizing car pools on a professional basis.

When Bill Harrison moved to the suburbs, he found there was no room in the neighborhood car pool, and the public transportation was so bad that he was always late for his city job. Primarily to solve his own problem, he came up with the idea of organizing a car pool, but it soon turned out to be a real money maker. He found that people were willing to pay to get into a car pool, and that he could easily supply the service.

What You Can Earn. Bill began running ads in the local newspapers and posting notices around town, announcing that he was looking for people willing to form car pools to go to various parts of the city each day, at various times. He was soon flooded with inquiries, and began getting the various groups together.

The only way to make money is to charge each rider a flat "finder's fee" for locating a car pool that will provide him with convenient transportation. Depending on local transportation conditions, you can set this fee as high as $20, although a somewhat lower fee will probably be more likely. Even at $10 a head, a half-dozen inquiries a week will net you $60 a week clear profit. This is about what Bill earns.

HOW TO BUILD YOUR WEALTH BASE

Here's What You Need.   You need absolutely nothing but a congested city nearby and limited public transportation. This, of course, describes almost every major city in the United States. Mass transportation is a problem of national concern.

How to Get Started.   Try to find out where the major employment centers are in the city, and approximately what time business starts in the morning. Also, scout the "bedroom" communities where people have a need for your car pool service. With this information, you are ready to promote the service.

How to Promote.   Use every bulletin board you can find—at the library, supermarket, church, lodge, bus depot and train station (if you can get away with it). Explain the service, and ask the readers to either call you or drop you a card with their requirements. Be sure to run ads in local newspapers, and try to get the editors to give you some free publicity. This kind of story makes good "copy" and they are often very pleased to take a swipe at buses and trains where service is deteriorating.

When you have enough names and localities, set up the schedules, and begin collecting your "finder's fees."

Your Opportunity for Growth.   Not much room to grow in this business. No one to our knowledge has ever made it a full-time operation but, run efficiently, it can be a steady source of income for many years.

CERAMIC SERVICES

Turn Clay into Money

Your Opportunity for Profit.   The arts and crafts bug bites most everyone at least once, and often the cure is sought at a local ceramic shop or studio. There, the prospective artist picks out a piece of greenware (an unfired clay article), and takes a few hours of instruction, then decorates and fires the piece. All this costs money for the ceramic hobbyist—money that can easily be yours when you become the neighborhood ceramic studio.

This is an easily learned craft that has retained its popularity over the years. You make money by giving lessons, selling greenware and decorating glazes and supplies, and by selling finished pieces much as a gift shop.

What You Can Earn.   Earnings in this business can vary a lot depending on how much time and money you want to invest. Perhaps the best way to start is to offer simple instruction in decorating the pieces, and to carry a limited selection of greenware for purchase by your students. Firing the pieces can be done by renting kiln time in a larger studio. As profits grow from this business, you will want to invest in your own kiln, and in the molds from which you can cast your own greenware.

Most basement hobbyists start this way, and then are surprised when the business takes off. Once you outgrow your own home, the next step to take is to open a full-time studio where you can offer lessons and supplies, in addition to a lucrative gift shop business handling a variety of lines. Such a studio can provide an income enjoyed only by a small percentage of people now working for a living.

HOW TO BUILD YOUR WEALTH BASE

Here's What You Need.   Many people have succeeded in this work with little or no art ability. This is one reason why the hobby is so popular with amateurs. If you have some talent along these lines, so much the better. Decorating, glazing, and firing are simple tasks that can be learned from the many publications available, or by taking a short course yourself at the adult school, or a big studio you hope to compete with some day. Don't be in a hurry to lay in a great deal of equipment in the beginning, either.
How to Get Started.   You can observe the business first hand by becoming a student at a studio. Once you're ready to branch out on your own, start looking for used equipment. Also check on the zoning requirements in your area. There are always ways of getting around sticky ordinances by calling yourself a teacher and running a class from your home. Usually, the town fathers will consider your operation similar to that of a music teacher who gives lessons in her home and will let you operate without trouble.
How to Promote.   Ads in the local newspaper can be effective. Use the headings called "instruction" in the classified pages. On occasion, you may want to try larger space ads when you have something special to offer—new courses starting, new molds, introductory rates, or what have you.

You can also put on demonstration-lectures for groups in town. If you offer a "group rate" at the end of the talk, you'll many times find that you have the makings of another course just from members of the group.
Your Opportunity for Growth.   If you want to grow, you'll quickly run out of space in the average home because you will need room to store larger amounts of molds and supplies, a growing stock of greenware, and storage of semi-finished pieces of your students between classes. Many people who start out this way very quickly find themselves in a full-time business operated out of a regular shop location.

CHAIR CANING

Making Money When the Bottom Falls Out

Your Opportunity for Profit. Our ancestors made some very beautiful furniture that is prized by collectors today. The caned-bottom chair is one of the most common pieces available, but only a museum piece might have the original caning. The caned seat must be replaced at intervals depending on how much the chair is used. Few collectors know how to replace damaged or worn out caning, and are usually willing to pay quite well for expert restoration.

Fortunately, it doesn't take long to become expert in this vanishing craft, and it can become a source of welcome income for someone with the time available.

What You Can Earn. Owners of antiques seldom quibble about the cost of a restoration. This does not mean you can charge outrageous prices. Rather, it means that you will get a very fair return on your time invested.

This is a service that can vary in price greatly depending where you live. In the New England area where antiques from this period are more common, you will find more competition and lower prices quoted. In Florida, competition might be much less and you could become the only expert in a certain area providing this service. It is not unusual to pay $20 or more for re-caning the seat of a single chair. An antique dining set with eight chairs can bring $150 or more.

An important fact to observe is this: it is not necessarily the smartest thing to do to cut your price to get the business. In this business you are working on a person's prized possession, and a "bargain" price can sometimes cost you a sale. In fact, this type of business sometimes can profit from a certain amount of "snob pricing." People like to tell how valuable their pieces are and how much it cost to have it expertly restored.

HOW TO BUILD YOUR WEALTH BASE

Here's What You Need.   By this time, you should have a good idea if this is the kind of business that would appeal to you. You have to enjoy working with your hands, have patience, and appreciate good craftsmanship in any kind of work.

There are mail-order houses that can supply you with all the instructions and materials you need. They can be found in the advertising columns of any number of handyman and hobby type magazines.

How to Get Started.   Practice first on a chair of your own. When you've finished, use it a while and you'll quickly discover what mistakes you may have made. Rip it out and do it over, or do a second chair. After about your third chair, you should be expert enough to tackle your first paying job.

How to Promote.   First, make a list of all the antique dealers in your area. Visit them and tell them of your service. You will be looking for two types of customers here: the dealer himself (to whom you will give a wholesale rate), and the customers that come to the dealer's shop.

Most dealers do not do any restoration work themselves, but contract out the work to professionals such as yourself. Try to get some of this work, and also try to get them to recommend you to their customers who may be looking for a repair job.

Another business builder is the classified pages of your telephone directory. Normally, this service is not even thought about until a need arises. Then a person will usually look to a source like the directory to find who in town does such work.

Your Opportunity for Growth.   Like many of the businesses previously discussed, you can grow in this business by aggressive selling and advertising, and going after all the business you can reasonably handle. However, if you get that interested, you should seriously consider broadening your restoration service—chair rushing, furniture refinishing, and actual repairs and replacement of broken or missing parts.

These skills are taught at adult schools, by correspondence, and in books. You should, by this time, have made friends with the local historical society. This will increase your contacts, and also help you broaden your knowledge of the whole business.

CHILDREN'S SHOWS

Perform for Profit

Your Opportunity for Profit.   Children are the ideal audience. They are delighted with familiar stories retold a hundred times, their vivid imaginations take the place of elaborate scenery or stage effects, and their enjoyment is not diluted if the performer is an amateur.

Children ask only one thing from a performer—that he have a genuine love of children and their make-believe world. If you have this quality (and what parent or grandparent doesn't?), you can become a producer or performer of children's shows.

What You Can Earn.   Your earning power is governed by the kind of show you can put on, your talent or experience, and the time you want to devote to the business. If, for example, magic is your hobby, you can easily charge $35 to $50 for an evening's entertainment.

The simplest way to charge is to find out what similar professional groups have charged. Use this figure as a baseline for scaling your fees. If you will be putting on a performance at which admission is to be charged, you might consider an arrangement whereby you receive a percentage of the total receipts. If you do this, make sure there is some fair minimum, below which your fee will not fall.

HOW TO BUILD YOUR WEALTH BASE

Here's What You Need.   What you will need, much more than talent, is the desire to make children happy. If you have some talent or experience in music, the theatre, puppetry, magic, or what have you—so much the better. However, the basic skills of entertaining children are easily acquired.

Here is a place where your local library can prove a real goldmine of information. Tell your librarian what you have in mind and you'll have trouble carrying home all the books that are available in this area.

How to Get Started.   If you have some particular talent, all you need do is decide on a show. If you're starting from scratch, then it would be wise to try your hand at a clown act, a puppet show, flannel board stories, and any other activities you think you might enjoy. The point is for *you* to find out your most comfortable role. Grease paint is a wonderful screen behind which an otherwise shy person can hide, and it's surprising how free you suddenly feel in front of a group when you are a clown, and not yourself.

If you still have doubts about your ability to entertain, then consider the sure-fire recorded puppet show. Most record stores carry stories for children—some of them acted out by a cast of professional actors, and including appropriate music and sound effects. Many of the classic fairy tales are available in such form.

Pick out some records, play them over to yourself, and visualize some easy scenery and stage action for a puppet show. Make some simple hand puppets to act out the story. All you do is move the puppets to conform to the action—the record does all the work of acting, music, and sound effects. If you transfer the record to a casette, you have an even easier way to carry your show.

How to Promote.   After you've gotten a routine fairly well rehearsed, put on a "free" show for some charitable group. This will be the best advertising you can get and it won't cost you anything but your time.

Make a list of all the organizations in town that use children's shows from time to time. Get in touch with them personally or with postcard mailers. The program secretary of a group is usually hard pressed to find program material.

Also, whenever you put on a show, make sure you have some sort of "programs" to pass out. The program should state that you are available for birthday parties and the like, and it should stress your moderate rates.

Your Opportunity for Growth. If you have a clown or magic act, you will be limited by your number of free hours, because only you can perform. As you acquire skill and a reputation, you can, of course, increase your charges. However, don't keep raising them to the point where you price yourself out of the market.

If you do puppet shows, where you as the mover of the performers are never actually seen, it is possible to expand to do other puppet shows on conflicting dates by using assistants. Make sure that they are as good as you before you send them out by themselves.

CLIPPING SERVICE

How to Turn Your Newspaper into Gold

Your Opportunity for Profit. A press-clipping service is a misunderstood business, and for this reason very few people think of it as an easy way to make money. People usually associate press clippings with movie stars and other famous people who want to collect notices and stories appearing about them in the press. Actually, they are a minor part of the business. Most successful press clipping services work for companies and organizations that have to keep up to date on matters reported in the daily papers.

For example: business firms eagerly seek out stories about their competitors as a clue to what they are doing. Private schools and colleges want to know about students who receive awards or prizes, so they can contact them about enrolling in their institution. Banks, insurance companies, and brokerage offices are constantly looking for new customers. What better way to get leads for salesmen than to find out who has been promoted to a bigger job?

You can add a whole list of clients like the above to your home clipping bureau. Your only investment consists of the daily papers and a pair of scissors. Each client tells you what his specific needs are, and you read the papers with these needs in mind. Every likely article or story is clipped, identified with a gummed sticker giving the name of the paper and the date, and then sent to the client on a regular basis.

What You Can Earn.   You are your client's newspaper reader. As a reader, you perform a service, even though you may find nothing of interest to clip in a particular issue. For this reason, you charge a monthly "reading fee," rather than so much a clipping.

Your reading fees will depend on the number of papers you scan, and the complexity of your client's needs. You're selling sharp eyes, common sense, and your time—so don't sell yourself too cheaply. Your minimum reading fee should be about $15 per month per client. This is about right if your reading covers a dozen or so of the bigger newspapers in your area. If your clients want statewide coverage, and you have to read more papers than this, then increase your reading fees. You can easily charge $50 a month for clients like this. A dozen or so clients can be handled with little investment in reading time and net you $300 to $500 a month.

HOW TO BUILD YOUR WEALTH BASE

Here's What You Need.   Subscribe to a dozen or so newspapers. Pick those papers which have particularly good coverage of business news. Your librarian can help you here. If you don't know the names of newspapers beyond your town, then check *Ayer's Guide* which lists all the newspapers and magazines in the country. Most libraries have a copy of this standard reference work.

Get a supply of gummed labels that you can attach to the top of each clipping you send to your clients. Either have them printed, or get a rubber stamp that includes space for the name of the publication and the date of issue, together with your own name and address.

How to Get Started.   The easiest way to get started is to make believe you have already signed up a number of clients, and clip items of interest to them. Label them and keep them in separate envelopes identified by client. Running this way for a week or two will tell you how much time it takes to scan the newspapers, and what newspapers are particularly productive of items.

How to Promote.   Once you have a fair number of clippings on a particular company, send that envelope to the owner or president with a short note telling him of your service, and giving a sample quotation for the monthly service.

You can also get a list of companies in your area and send them a regular direct mail piece soliciting inquiries. Those that are interested are followed up by a personal call. Once your business gets somewhat larger, you should invest in regular advertising in the classified pages of your telephone directory.

Your Opportunity for Growth.   This business can grow far beyond your local area both in the newspapers you read and the clients you service. Many national corporations are interested in having news items clipped relating to their personnel or competitors that are located in your area. Also, because you can get newspapers from all over the country, you can service clients all over the country by mail.

Help for expansion is easy to get for this business. Right now you can probably name a half dozen friends who would be willing to work for you a few hours each morning reading newspapers. If you charge fairly for your services, you'll be able to pay these helpers, and devote your time to getting more customers and building your business to greater potentials.

You can also add this service to other businesses described in this book—advertising services, mailing services, and free-lance researcher.

COLLECTION SERVICE

Collect for Others and Make Money for Yourself

Your Opportunity for Profit.   It isn't unusual for businessmen to have problems collecting money from time to time. More often than not, the people who owe the money take the attitude that "the squeaky wheel is the one that gets the oil." That is, the one who hollers most is the one who gets paid. Most businessmen do not like to holler," and often prefer to turn their collections over to someone else to handle on a less personal basis. If you don't mind the guff that sometimes comes with a sticky collection, this can be a profitable business.

What You Can Earn.   It is impossible for us to give you any money examples that would be meaningful to every reader. Often, states regulate the amount that a collection agency can charge. But, in almost all cases, the fee is based on a percentage of the amount to be collected, and here is how it works:

- You get the amount owed, and the name and address of the person owing the money.
- The person to whom the money is owed agrees to let you keep a fixed percentage of what you collect.
- After you collect, you deposit the check in *your* business account. After the check clears, you pay the proceeds, less your fee, to the person who hired you.

An active collection agency in a moderate sized community can do well, and we have heard of them returning as high as $20,000 a year for a reasonable amount of activity. Many collection agencies work by mail exclusively, and can therefore service a much larger area.

HOW TO BUILD YOUR WEALTH BASE

Here's What You Need. Most important of all, you need the kind of personality that isn't easily bruised when someone slams a door in your face. You must be persistent. Other than that, you will need only some means of keeping accurate accounts books, and a business bank account. You should really consider having at least a part-time secretary to handle calls, finances and records. Perhaps your wife could start the office service business described in this book to help, and make some money of her own.

How to Get Started. First, check at either your local city hall, or the county seat to see if there are any regulations governing a collection service in your area. In some cases, you will have to be bonded. Even if it is not required, consider it as a sign of responsibility to your clients. Also determine if local codes regulate the amounts you can charge. After you have discovered and complied with all necessary regulations, have a simple card printed and mailed to every business in your area. Every business has a need for this service at one time or another, and you should get as broad an exposure as possible. You might call on all the accountants in your area. They are often well aware of who owes who money, but they seldom do more than write letters.

How to Promote. Other than the direct contact we mentioned, the best bet is to run an ad in the classified part of your local phone directory. You can also try to run an ad in any local newsletters of businessmen and CPA's.

Your Opportunity for Growth. You will profit in direct proportion to your persistence. As you collect from the "tough" ones, your reputation will spread among other businessmen and you will get more assignments.

Remember, if you plan to add to your staff, those you consider must have the same temperament as yourself. Like most service businesses, which are built on the personality of the owner, it will be hard to find someone who can be as effective as you in a short time. Plan to train someone, and be patient. It will be worth it in the long run.

You might even use your part-time secretary to do some of the initial calls for collection. These calls should be gentle reminders until you come in with the full authority of your service.

CORD WOOD SUPPLY BUSINESS

You Earn While They Burn

Your Opportunity for Profit.   Fireplaces have always been popular in homes. And, where you have a fireplace, you obviously have a need for wood. If you've ever fed a fireplace of your own, you'll realize how quickly it can go through a pile of firewood. Supplying this wood can be a fairly profitable spare time business, even if you don't own a tree.

What You Can Earn.   Firewood is sold by the "cord." This is the amount of wood in a pile 4 feet wide, 4 feet high, and 8 feet long. In some parts of the country, this is sold for $50, delivered. Be sure to "shop" your competition for the local price range.

You can sell the wood delivered and stacked at your customer's door, or the customer can come to your place of business and pick up the wood himself. You can charge more for the first, but the second gives you less work and eliminates the need for a pick-up truck. Clean, white birch logs usually sell for more than other woods, because people like them for their decorative value.

HOW TO BUILD YOUR WEALTH BASE

Here's What You Need.   Your main need is for a good supply of wood. One way of getting this is to offer to fell trees and cart away the wood for builders. Usually, builders bulldoze the trees out of the way and then have to spend additional money to have them carted away. You can make money hauling the wood, and make even more money when you cut it up for sale. If you have access to a patch of woods, you have another source of supply.

A chain saw, sledge hammer, and wedges are all the tools you will need.

How to Get Started. Keep a sharp eye out for builders who are developing large tracts in wooded areas. Arrange to clear the wood for a price. Then cut it up in fireplace lengths—2 feet. The ideal way to work the business is to eliminate the hauling to your storage area, and the re-loading and shipping to your customer. Actually, this is not hard to do at all.

Simply work on a "back order" basis. That is, don't promise delivery to customers for at least two weeks. This gives you the time to scout the wood, cut it, and deliver directly, without ever having to store it.

How to Promote. Classified ads are about your best bet. If you own property and can run a business from the side of the road, a good sign will get you business from passing motorists. Make sure that your phone number is prominent on this sign. Some people will not want to load their car trunks with wood, and will prefer to phone you to arrange for delivery.

The doormen at elegant city apartments often run a cord wood service for tenants—at extremely high prices. You can sell to these "middlemen"—at prices higher than you would ordinarily charge in the suburbs.

Your Opportunity for Growth. Once you have people stopping at your place for wood, you can add other lines—fencing materials, seasonal decorations, and the like, depending on your inclinations. Also, you can consider making a double profit on your wood. You simply offer a tree trimming service—for which you charge the customer—then re-sell the wood you have just cut out.

As you deliver the wood, you may notice the perfect place for a patio to be built. Be sure to call this to your customer's attention. It's an ideal way to kick off another new business.

CURB AND MAILBOX
STENCIL SERVICE

Introduce Yourself to Loads of Customers

Your Opportunity for Profit.   This is a business where you make money by giving something away! Every house should have the street number easily visible from the road. What better place is there to put this number but on the curb next to the driveway? Boy Scout troops sometimes do this as a fund raising project, and if you think you'll find yourself in conflict with their program, just forget this. But, if you want an easy way to meet loads of customers for your other businesses, then this device can be just the trick.

True, you can charge 50 cents to a dollar for stenciling a street number on a curb or a mailbox, and quickly earn a couple of hundred dollars in an average town working a couple of weekends. We suggest, however, that you do it *free* as a means of introducing yourself and your other services to potential customers.

What You Can Earn.   For once, it's really impossible to put a figure on your earning potential here. It all depends on what other businesses you may be using to build your personal Wealth Base. As you go through this book, you'll discover dozens of business opportunities which require a face-to-face contact with your customer. If you go up and ask a homeowner if he would like his house number stenciled free on the curb, it's highly unlikely he will refuse.

After you've done the job, leave a simple brochure or flyer describing your other services. While you're stenciling the number, you can even size up the potential and be ready to suggest to the customer that he consider having his driveway sealed, or have his air-conditioner removed for the winter, have his lawn attended to by a professional, or his swimming pool cleaned and tested. These and many other businesses are described throughout this book and are ideal to tie into this free "business."

HOW TO BUILD YOUR WEALTH BASE

Here's What You Need.   Your investment in this business won't exceed a few dollars. Stenciling kits are available in department stores and paint shops. The stencil is easily changed to different numbers, and you use it with a handy aerosol can of paint.

Your most important need, however, is a flyer of some sort that you can leave with your customer. You might plan on giving away some specialty item like a calendar or memo pad with your name and business address. It gets more attention than just mailing it to prospects.

How to Get Started.   Make sure you're prepared with flyers that completely tell the story you have in mind. Be ready with names and addresses of satisfied customers, too. If you're using this device to sell your driveway sealing service, for example, be ready to tell who in the immediate neighborhood has used you.

With this homework done, all you need is the stencil kit.

How to Promote.   There is only one way to promote this business. You walk up to a door, ring the bell, and tell the homeowner that you will stencil his house number on the curb as a free, no-strings attached service. Once he says "yes," do the job quickly and then come back with your main story.

Your Opportunity for Growth.   Again, your opportunity for growth will depend on what other businesses you are cultivating. If your "story" can be told quickly and completely in a flyer, then you might consider having some young helpers do the actual stenciling and distributing of flyers for you. You can pay them on some fair basis out of the profits of your real business.

DANCING LESSONS

Dance Your Way to Success

Your Opportunity for Profit.   You've met them at parties—the couple who dance well and enjoy what they are doing. Often, they delight in helping their friends become better dancers by showing them new steps.

This couple can have the best of two worlds—having fun while working on building their Wealth Base. They can make money without any significant investment. The secret of success in this business lies in the use of other people's homes, so expensive studio overhead expenses are eliminated.

What You Can Earn.   This is a business where you can quickly establish a price. Simply inquire at nearby dance studios and ask for a schedule of their charges. Their prices include overhead—something you don't have. Because you will have none of these charges draining away earnings, you can often quote prices averaging only half those of a regular studio.

If the studio charges $100 for a series of lessons, offer the same number for $50. You can increase your average earnings by giving lessons to groups at a discount. Even a neighborhood bridge club can be a prospect for such an offer. They get together for social evenings with cards; it would be natural to extend their social activity by an activity such as dancing.

HOW TO BUILD YOUR WEALTH BASE

Here's What You Need.   Obviously, you will need to know how to dance, and to be able to teach others what you enjoy doing. Beyond this, all you'll need is a good selection of dance records and a record player.

Ask your music store to show you a special record player commonly used in dance studios. It is designed for frequent needle lifting without danger of scratching the record.

How to Get Started. The key to success in this business lies in your use of other people's homes, or places where they meet as a group. It is a good idea to begin by locating groups that meet regularly—the PTA, church, lodge, civic, and social groups are good examples. Contact members you might know in each group, and send out short notes announcing your service to them.

Put together a little "show" than can demonstrate the kind of dances you and your partner will teach the group. Then pick several members of the group who say they have "no talent at all" and show how easy it is to learn simple steps.

These sample dances should be geared to the group you're dealing with. Far-out fads seldom go over with the older, more conservative group. Apply the business discovery that assures success —*supply a need.*

How to Promote. You should be able to offer a variety of programs to allow your clients some selection. Offer various combinations of dances and numbers of lessons at different prices. Spell these out in a simple folder or brochure that you can pass out whenever you're asked to explain your service to some group.

You also can benefit from small, regular ads in the classified sections of your local newspaper. Try using the "personal" columns rather than those headed "dance instruction." Another way to get things going is to perform your "show" at some local affair as a bazaar, fair, or social evening.

Your Opportunity for Growth. Because there are virtually no overhead costs in this "non-studio" dance instruction business, you might never want to open a studio, however big your business becomes. But, a studio does offer some advantages. Namely, it allows you to have an operation going all day with the help of hired teachers. And, if you can get good dance instructors, you can have the closest thing to a "business annuity"—giving ballet lessons to young children.

DECORATIVE CANDLE MAKING

Light Up Your Future

Your Opportunity for Profit.   Whenever you see a festive table setting, you're sure to notice that candles form an important part of the decorative scheme. Simple, store-bought candles in candlesticks are sometimes adequate, but there are many times when nothing but a large, decorated candle will carry out the spirit of the occasion. This is particularly true around the holidays, when parties are most likely to be given.

Making decorative candles can be both fun and profitable. The materials are inexpensive, and the craft is easily learned. Molds to form the candles can be improvised from a number of common household objects, such as milk cartons and a variety of empty plastic bottles.

What You Can Earn.   A large, eight-inch decorated candle can easily sell for $3 at retail. Yet, the materials involved—wax, wicking and dyes—cost only a fraction of this amount. If you wish, you can use candle making as an enjoyable hobby that pays for itself, and as solid help to build your personal Wealth Base.

You can work out a system that will enable you to turn out fairly large quantities of finished candles that will find a ready market in gift shops, florists, department and variety stores. With imaginative marketing, the business can be expanded to a full-time, high income producing business.

This is a manufacturing business and you should gradually build up an investment in finished goods. Candles don't spoil, shrink, or go out of style. You can control your inventory at any level, depending on your sales experience.

HOW TO BUILD YOUR WEALTH BASE

Here's What You Need.   You should enjoy working with your hands, and also have a convenient place in which to work. If you've never made your own candles, then a research trip to the library is in order. The craft is simple: you choose your mold and run a piece of wicking up the middle. Melted wax is poured into the mold, and when cool, you have a candle that you can further decorate with sequins and other decorative elements. Holiday issues of women's magazines usually carry articles on candle making, and once you've made a few according to directions, you'll find it easy to come up with your own original designs.

How to Get Started.   First, make up some samples. Display these at a meeting of a women's club, or church fair, and you will be on your way. At meetings such as these, make sure you have available for hand-out a simple description of your service and products.

How to Promote.   Next, you should call on the owner of every gift and variety shop in town that carries mass-produced candles. In the beginning, you can suggest handling your special candles on consignment. This represents no risk to the owner of the store. He simply places your merchandise on display with his other items. If he makes a sale, he keeps part of the proceeds and gives the rest to you. If no sales are made, you take back your candles and it costs him nothing.

Your Opportunity for Growth.   You'll find that most of your sales will come around the holiday season. Fortunately, you can work all summer building up a supply to meet this demand without having to work 24 hours a day during your busy selling season. The business can grow in proportion to the time you want to invest in building and selling your inventory. The business is ideal for a husband and wife team, because there is an easy division of labor—one person makes the candles and the other decorates them.

DOG GROOMING AND BOARDING

Pets Mean Profits for You

Your Opportunity for Profit.   Pets are part of the family, and those who really care for them will spend quite a bit of money to see that they look and feel well. To look well, many people depend on professional dog grooming services, and you can become part of this growing field with a little practice and a few inexpensive tools.

Some dogs require constant attention; the grooming of a large sheep dog can take half a day. Even the smaller dogs can require a lot of attention. Consider the extent to which people go to have a toy poodle clipped. Once clipped, the poodle must be attended to at least once a month, or it begins to resemble a mutt.

What You Can Earn.   You should establish basic prices for the various services you can offer:

- Clipping
- Special trimming—poodle trims, etc.
- Nail trimming
- Bathing
- Skin and coat treatments
- and any special services a pet owner might request

Obviously, clipping a sheep dog will take much longer than a trim of a small fox terrier. Figure what your time is worth (remember Chapter 1) and set the rate as you size up the dog. It is not uncommon to charge as much as $50 to bathe and comb out a large sheep dog. To make sure you are in line, check a nearby pet store offering similar services. Because of large regional differences, it is almost impossible to give money figures that would be meaningful to all readers.

HOW TO BUILD YOUR WEALTH BASE

Here's What You Need.   First of all, you will need to know how to handle animals, and how to do the trimming and bathing in a professional way. If you have raised a dog of your own, you've got a start, but if you have no experience, take a job in a kennel for as long as it is necessary to learn the craft. One of the top Hollywood dog trainers began her career this way, and now has a thriving animal training and care business.

You will also need some basic equipment: curry combs, shears, brushes, and the space to work. A converted garage, with running water for bathing, and heat for winter comfort will fit the bill nicely.

How to Get Started.   Everyone has a few friends who own dogs. You can offer to trim and clip them, without charge, as an "introductory" offer. After this, they will become steady customers, and will refer their friends to you. Be sure to make yourself known to any local kennel clubs, and any animal breeders groups in the area.

How to Promote.   If the local pet store does not offer a similar service, you can offer to work for him, at your place, on a referral basis. Every time he sends you a customer, you simply extend him a commission for his help. Often 10% to 20% will suffice to get an enthusiastic pet shop owner working for you.

You might run classified ads, if your paper has a "pets and livestock" column. Be sure to get the roster of members of the local kennel clubs and send them regular announcements of various services.

Your Opportunity for Growth.   You can expand this service in a variety of directions: Training obedience classes, boarding (both at your kennels, and on a referral basis to owners of similar animals), and finally a full service pet shop. If you live in a large metropolitan area, you might consider becoming the "specialist." Many earn considerable sums by becoming the "poodle professionals," "sheep-dog professionals," etc.

DRAFTING SERVICE

Draw Yourself a Bright Future

Your Opportunity for Profit.   To work as a skilled and highly-paid draftsman requires years of study and experience. Yet, the knowledge required to run your own drafting service is really minimal, even though you will be contracting to do some very complicated work for engineering and technical companies near you.

You can do this successfully and profitably by using the experience of others—the very same draftsmen and designers who work for these companies, and who will do the actual drafting work.

Most companies that hire engineers and draftsmen keep a minimum staff usually to keep their overhead down. When work piles up, and overtime can't solve the problem in time, then they will go outside for temporary help. Here's where you step in to reap the profits.

Tom Harris did this, and he runs what is actually a miniature "job shop." That is, he has a list of available draftsmen in his area who are anxious to make some part-time money. He farms the work out to them, and they are the ones who actually do the drafting. He does the selling and collects the profits. In fact, he made over $22,000 in his second year of operation.

What You Can Earn. Setting an hourly rate for your drafting service will mean a little digging for information on your part. Rates vary across the country for similar work. A fair rule of thumb is to find out the hourly rate paid to experienced draftsmen by the companies you will be contacting for work, and then raise this rate by about 75%. If the going rate for draftsmen is $4.50 an hour, your price should be between $7.50 and $8 an hour. This may sound high, but remember that this expense is the total cost to the company. They have no extra expenses in the form of fringe benefits, or what have you to add to this price. It actually works out cheaper than overtime for them.

HOW TO BUILD YOUR WEALTH BASE

Here's What You Need. Initially, you will be acting as a drafting "broker." You will be supplying a drafting service, but doing little, if any at all, yourself. You won't need an office, but a telephone answering service will help. The draftsmen who do the work for you will be working in their own homes with their own equipment, so you won't need any expensive items or furniture.

How to Get Started. If you have any drafting experience, you will have a good idea of who your first customers should be. Civil engineers, manufacturers, local and state engineering departments, and consulting engineers are sources you should contact first. Don't overlook lawyers. Many times they need precision drawings for patent applications, or for presentation to a court in cases involving property rights, negligence, and so on.

Check the yellow pages of your phone directory and make a list of all the companies that could possibly use your service. Then phone each company and ask the switchboard operator for the name of the chief draftsman. Knowing his name will help you when you make your proposal in person.

You will also need to build a staff of "stringers." These are the draftsmen who will actually do the work. You can find them through friends, asking at drafting supply houses and blueprinters, and even by running a small classified ad in your local newspaper.

How to Promote.   Direct contact is really the key to big jobs. Call on the chief draftsmen and tell them of your service and the various drafting talents represented on your "staff." Under no circumstances should you reveal the actual names of the people who work for you.

Your Opportunity for Growth.   Some of the most successful technical houses started out by being small job-shops. One successful operator we know of started this way, and now runs a very profitable business. He has expanded his service to include personnel recruitment in the technical areas, and has plans for even more diversified activities in the future.

As you grow, you will find opportunities that your own experience will tell you are ones to exploit. Supplying just the drafting materials—pencils, paper, and drafting furniture and supplies—is just one thought. You can come up with many more.

FISH TANK CLEANING

A Watery Way to Wealth

Your Opportunity for Profit.   Most people snicker when we tell them of this opportunity, but consider this: every pet store has dozens of large tanks for their tropical fish. These tanks must be kept clean and spotless if customers are to be impressed.

Thousands of people across the country keep rather large home aquariums, and have the same problem of maintenance. And the hobby is growing. Many offices are using aquaria as decorative elements. Apart from a quick wipe on the outside of the tank, you won't find the night-cleaning man getting involved in fish tank cleaning. So you see—a real opportunity exists for one of those profitable, specialized service businesses that has virtually no competition.

What You Can Earn.   Your charges are based on standard tank sizes—which range from 2 to 125 gallons. Since the glass area of the tank is roughly proportional to the amount of water the tank holds, you can base your price on gallonage of the tank. At 5 cents a gallon, cleaning a standard 55 gallon tank earns you $2.75.

A nearby tropical fish store has a total of 1230 gallons of display fish tanks, all of them in need of regular cleaning. You could make $61.50 every time you serviced this store.

HOW TO BUILD YOUR WEALTH BASE

Here's What You Need.   You need a few tools to get started in this business, but the total investment is quite reasonable. Your cleaning kit consists of a good quality window squeegee, a small vacuum pump and some rubber tubing, and a dip tube tank cleaner. The *vacuum* pump is not the same as the *air* pump commonly used to pump air into fish tanks. The squeegee is a simple hardware store item. The rest of the things can be bought by mail from aquarium supply houses that regularly advertise in the pages of fish hobbyist magazines.

How to Get Started.   Start by making friends with the local pet store owners. Not only can they be customers for your new service, but they can also put you in touch with their customers who are serious about their hobby and can be likely prospects for regular tank cleaning services.

At the same time, find out if there is a local club of fish fanciers. It would be worth a few dollars to join the club simply for the contacts that can be made through such a group.

Helpful hint on cleaning: when cleaning tanks, start by gently vacuuming up the debris that accumulates on the bottom of the tank. Then clean the insides of the tank with the squeegee, working it carefully from the bottom to the top of the tank. Wipe the squeegee with a rag, and repeat until done. Be careful you don't disturb the plant arrangements or other display that the owner has worked up.

How to Promote.   This is the kind of business that is "kooky" enough to get you some free publicity in your local newspaper. Once you've gotten enough experience to call yourself something of an expert, get in touch with the editor. Your business should appeal to his sense of human interest news, and the resulting publicity will bring you a lot of business.

As you work with pet shops, try to get them to display some small announcement of your service near their tanks of tropical fish.

Your Opportunity for Growth.   As soon as possible try to establish a route similar to ones used by any service business. A few dollars here, and a few dollars there, may seem like a hard way to accumulate money. But remember, if you can handle a dozen or so customers on a Saturday by making a loop that cuts down traveling time and distance, you'll wind up home $50 to $100 richer at the end of the day.

Eventually, like many of the other "growth" businesses described in this book, you may want to hire assistants to do the actual work, while you concentrate on this and other ways of building your Wealth Base.

FLOWER ARRANGING

A Bouquet of Profits

Your Opportunity for Profit.   If people admire your garden and the floral arrangements you create for your own parties, then the chances are that you have the talent to make money in your spare time doing the things you enjoy most.

Making money in flowers is normally thought to be the work of a florist. Yet, a part-timer such as yourself can earn money in this fascinating field in several ways without the expense of opening a store yourself. You can, for example:

- work *with* a local florist, giving him vitally needed help during his peak periods
- or if you wish, you can provide most of the services of the florist, working from your own home.

What You Can Earn.   Considering the cost of the basic materials of a floral display or bouquet, most of what you charge will be profit.

It is not unusual to earn $100 or more on a single wedding job. The work is enjoyable, and once your reputation gets around, very little selling will have to be done. Actual prices will have to be worked out depending on the cost of materials and the time you spend on the design and arrangements.

HOW TO BUILD YOUR WEALTH BASE

Here's What You Need.   Obviously, you have to like to work with flowers. If you need the confidence that comes with training, you might want to check some of the courses given in this field. Many times, the local adult education classes in your town include classes in flower arranging. Or, if you want to study by mail, the various flower magazines carry ads from schools that offer this training.

Flowers are your basic material and you get them from your own garden, or from a wholesale florist. Flower arranging supplies are available at florists, garden supply shops, and by mail.

How to Get Started. After you've gotten your materials together, think of the various ways floral displays are used within your immediate circle of friends. In your lists of prospects, don't forget to include the banquet manager at your local hotel, and the managers of the various restaurants—particularly those catering to parties.

If you plan to work with a florist, a phone call will undoubtedly get you a warm welcome—particularly if you call a short time before the busy season.

How to Promote. Make a few displays for your immediate group to get the word around about your new business. A church supper featuring a few of your floral centerpieces will get you an amount of free publicity impossible to buy in any other fashion.

Your best advertising will be in the form of referrals. Therefore, you should call on hotel and banquet managers and show them how you can help make meetings they cater more successful with floral displays. Make yourself known to ministers, funeral directors, and others who can suggest your services to others. Don't forget the luncheon secretary of the many clubs and societies in your town.

Your Opportunity for Growth. With the type of advertising you'll be doing the business will grow slowly at first, then begin to rise more sharply as you become known. At some point, you'll either have to turn away business because your spare time won't permit any more work, or you'll have to go full-time, and consider the possibility of opening a flower shop.

Keep in mind that about a third of the shops are owned and operated by women. Here is an ideal husband and wife business opportunity.

You will be visiting homes a lot in this business. Here is an ideal opportunity to add other services—interior decorating, party consultant, and a host of others.

FREE-LANCE RESEARCHER

Find Profits for Yourself

Your Opportunity for Profit. "Time is money." Benjamin Franklin said this a long time ago, and no one will argue the fact. *Information* is also money, and the time it takes to get it can be your key to a very profitable business: free-lance researcher.

For example: The authors of this book had to research out hundreds of facts and case histories relating to the businesses described. Without this research, the book simply could not be written. Not only writers, but businessmen, too, need help with all sorts of projects.

Consider the needs of a manufacturer who wants the names of all the sales managers of certain types of companies in a given area. He would have to spend hours with a commercial directory in order to do it. It is often more costly in terms of salary, overhead, and lost time from the job, to assign the job to a regular employee. This is where you can step in to make money for yourself.

What You Can Earn. This sort of professional research work is usually charged according to the actual time spent. It is not uncommon to charge $4 to $7 an hour for even simple work. For example: a large manufacturer wanted to know the names and addresses of all his competitors in the United States. They knew where these names were to be found, and even had a complete set of directories available. But, they couldn't afford to tie up a clerk to do the job. At $4 an hour, a free-lance researcher made almost $50 for a little more than a day's work.

HOW TO BUILD YOUR WEALTH BASE

Here's What You Need. You need nothing but the time. All the research will be done among sources either supplied by your client or readily available in the library. What is essential, however, is a personality that enjoys digging out details, and takes pride in doing accurate work.

How to Get Started. Get in touch with the following types of businesses because they are most likely to use your services:

- mailing list compilers
- letter shops and mailing houses
- retail stores (especially those using direct mail)
- local manufacturers (particularly of industrial products)
- advertising agencies
- generally, any type of business that goes after specialized customers

If you live near any large city, add fund-raising organizations to the above list. They often use outside help in lining up prospects for donations.

Write to your prospects. Outline your service as a custom research business that is able to collect and record information on a wide variety of topics.

How to Promote. Once you've written to the companies you've selected, follow up with a phone call about a week later. Try, at this point, to get a personal interview. This is not the kind of service that can be sold immediately with a single letter or phone call. What you want to do is to establish a line of communication with someone important. Then, when a job needs doing, you'll be the one they will think of immediately.

Your Opportunity for Growth. The best way to grow in this business is to follow the path of other firms that are now well-established in the business. Work hard to add more clients, and always be on the lookout for people who can do the actual work for you. As you grow, spend less time working on projects yourself, and spend more time lining up new clients.

Once you have acquired something of a reputation and have a string of fairly regular clients, you might just find yourself behind the desk of your own private office running a very lucrative full-time business.

If you find yourself making many copies of reports for clients, you might consider buying a mimeograph machine, and offering duplicating as an additional service.

FREE-LANCE SECRETARY

"Take a Letter" Really Means "Take Profits for You"

Your Opportunity for Profit.   Modern business simply couldn't operate without the services of the millions of full-time secretaries in offices all over the land. But—who performs the secretarial services for the small businessman who doesn't need a full-time secretary, or the executive who is traveling away from his office and needs reports or letters to be finished as soon as possible?

You—the free-lance secretary, can do this job and earn a lot more, on an hourly basis, than you would working a nine-to-five job in the office. You are really an independent business person, running a business that can be as small or as big as your time permits. This is an ideal opportunity for an "ex-secretary" who left a full-time job to become a full-time homemaker, and now finds some free hours in her day that can earn her money.

What You Can Earn.   First, look in the want-ads and find out what experienced secretaries are earning in your locality. The rates vary so much in various parts of the country, that it's impossible to give a figure here. Take the weekly rate for an experienced secretary and double it. Then figure out how much this comes to on an hourly basis. This is what you should charge for your time. If a good secretary can earn $140 for a 35-hour week in your area, you should charge $280 for the same hours, or $8 an hour.

In addition to straight charges for your time, you'll quickly find ways to earn extra money for related services. Mimeographing reports is one such service. Elsewhere in this book are detailed instructions on setting up a mimeographing service. And, of course, you can offer straight manuscript typing services, not only to businessmen, but to students, writers, and others needing publication quality typing.

How quickly a business like this can mushroom into something big is illustrated by the case of Mrs. Beth Benson. She began her service with typing simple letters, envelopes, and reports. In little over a year, virtually by word of mouth advertising alone, her volume of work grew to such an extent that she had to rent an office and part-time helpers to handle the overflow of work.

With an office, she added the duplicating services, plus a telephone answering service, and a transcription service. She rents dictating machines and makes regular pickups of the recordings for typing later on. Her income is over $10,000 a year after all expenses are paid—and she spends only a few hours a day supervising her helpers.

HOW TO BUILD YOUR WEALTH BASE

Here's What You Need. You will need the basic secretarial skills. If your shorthand is a little rusty, don't worry too much. Most of your work in the beginning will probably be typing and related services. Later on, you can hire a helper who can do swift accurate work from dictating machines. A typewriter in good condition is a must. Think about an electric machine that uses the black carbon ribbons. Usually, you can rent a machine for a reasonable sum a month and then apply your payments toward purchase later on.

How to Get Started. Set up a schedule of charges that you can quote to prospective clients. Set aside a room as your office. This is vital if you are to do quick, accurate work. Lugging out the typewriter each time you need it and then trying to type on the dining room table is to invite disaster. Be businesslike about your business.

How to Promote.   Take Mrs. Benson's advice and use the word-of-mouth route as your first advertising medium. Let the various groups in town know you're in business, and a goodly number of inquiries will soon come your way. Work with the various service organizations in town (the membership is heavy with small businessmen) and you will get numerous leads. Also, make sure you call on the manager of any nearby hotels. Many times a traveling businessman will ask the hotel management for local secretarial help.

Finally, like Mrs. Benson, you can use small ads in the telephone directory, because this is the place where someone looking for such service will, in all likelihood, look first.

Your Opportunity for Growth.   This business can grow into a full-scale business employing many people on a full- or part-time basis. It all depends on how many hours you want to spend in making the business grow. If you add the various other services associated with secretarial work, the income can really mount up.

FREE-TIME BARTENDING

Be a Money Mixer

Your Opportunity for Profit.   Are you a "good mixer"—with people as well as with drinks? If so, this opportunity in bartending can be just the thing to make odd hours productive. The work is not hard, pays fairly well, and is almost always an evening or weekend job that doesn't interfere with your regular work.

Most commercial bars and restaurants have their own regular

staff, so don't waste time here. However, you can build up a good list of clients by contacting the local fraternal and veterans' clubs that have bars, and by getting a reputation with the well-to-do people in town who throw big parties. Get a name for yourself, and you'll always be in demand by party givers trying to outdo each other.

What You Can Earn. Joe Callahan is a mailman in an Eastern town. He wanted to add to his income and hit upon the idea of tending bar at the local American Legion Hall to which he belonged. Previously, members had shared the job and disliked doing it. The members now share the cost of Joe's services, which makes him about $50 richer each week.

A good bartender who specializes in social affairs of the wealthy can often make over $50 for a single party. Most jobs should be quoted on an hourly rate with a clear understanding of the hours you will work, provisions for relief, overtime, and so on. Another thing to watch out for are union regulations, and any state or local licensing requirements. Usually these laws apply only to work in commercial bars, and not to bartenders working private homes or clubs.

HOW TO BUILD YOUR WEALTH BASE

Here's What You Need. A great asset for any bartender is a good ear for listening, particularly if the party is a big one. Everyone carries on conversations, mostly one-way, with bartenders, which get longer as the evening wears on.

Of course, you should keep handy a copy of a mixed-drink guide in case someone asks for an out-of-the-ordinary drink.

How to Get Started. If you can mix a drink, and your friends know it, you're halfway there. Simply tell them you are available for parties and other functions. Next, start looking around at the local organizations with bars in their meeting places. You might even check with the temporary employment agencies. They often have calls for party help, and a bartender's spot is often the hardest one to fill.

How to Promote. Building your reputation, and direct contact with likely prospects, are the two best ways to build your income from this business. Around holidays, when parties are in full swing, you might experiment by running a small ad or two in your newspaper.

You might also consider sending an announcement card to people who give parties. It's easy to find out who they are—simply read the social pages of your newspaper and build a list of prospects. This kind of prospecting can pay off quite handsomely.

Your Opportunity for Growth.   You're only one man and you only have so many hours to spend at this work. If you find that your promoting has built up so many calls for your service, you might consider adding helpers to take up the excess. You might even get to the point where you do none of the work yourself, but merely supply the help.

In such a case, you would be acting as an employment agency. Check the regulations regarding the licensing of employment agencies in your area, before you get too deeply involved in supplying employees to others.

You might consider tying in with a "Party Consultant," as we have described in this book, or even taking on the job yourself as an avenue of profitable expansion. The "team" approach is an ideal husband-and-wife business.

FUND RAISER

Raising Money for Others
Puts Money in Your Pocket

Your Opportunity for Profit.   There are quite a few large companies which specialize in the raising of funds for charities, churches and fraternal organizations. They are very effective, but, for the most part, they limit their services to larger clients.

Knowing this fact can put you into a pleasant, and profitable business. After all, just about every non-profit group in town has a fund-raising drive at least once a year. For the most part, they are headed by volunteers with little feel for the raising of money. If you have any sales experience and like the organization work that goes into building a team, this is the business for you.

As the local fund raiser, you do not actually go out and solicit the funds—you organize, train and direct the membership in the work of gathering money.

What You Can Earn. You can charge a fixed percentage of the total amount you raise for a group. For this very professional help, it is not uncommon to charge 15 to 25%. Of course, it is common to guarantee a certain figure, and reduce the fee a small amount if the drive does not meet the quota. For this reason, you must carefully estimate the quota. Be sure to request the results of previous drives so that you have some basis for the estimate.

You might encounter some resistance to the percentage arrangement. It is not uncommon for some organizations to resent that your pay increases as they give more. The alternative, and it is the way the big consultants work, is to charge a flat fee, based on the time and effort involved. Here, you should use the methods described in Chapter 1 to determine your fee.

HOW TO BUILD YOUR WEALTH BASE

Here's What You Need. You need nothing more than a good sales sense and an ability to handle a lot of detail. Several good books are available outlining techniques of fund raising. You might have to hire a temporary secretary for some jobs, but you should figure charging her salary off as a direct expense to the organization.

How to Get Started. Make a list of every group in your neighborhood who could use this kind of help: churches, scouts, lodges, community service organizations, and other special interest, nonprofit groups. Then either call on each personally, or write a dignified, but hard-selling letter describing your service. Be sure to emphasize your selling and management ability.

How to Promote. The ultimate number of clients you can service is quite small, so about the best methods of promotion are direct mail and direct contact. Of course, as you gain experience and a reputation, word of mouth will begin to be your best salesman.

Your Opportunity for Growth.   Remember, you do not actually do any of the canvassing. You plan and run the drives, using the groups' membership as the actual fund collectors. This means that it is possible for you to run more than one campaign at a time. But, be careful that you do not let the second assignment interfere with a present one. After all, word of mouth advertising can work adversely, too. The best way to expand is to either take on an associate with similar talents, or form a partnership with someone who already has built up a "practice." You might also form an alliance with a local advertising or public relations agency. The benefit here is that they will help you with any graphics and writing, and could offer, in return, assistance in helping you develop your business.

When you've gotten some reputation in this area, you can put on seminars for people interested in raising money. It is not uncommon to charge several hundred dollars *per registrant* for a program lasting several days.

GARAGE-SALE CONSULTANT

Open Wide the Door to Profits

Your Opportunity for Profit.   A garage sale is a popular way of getting rid of the clutter that has a way of accumulating in every house. But, to most people, organizing such a sale is a chore. So the junk continues to accumulate.

Beverly Small came up with the idea of offering to take over this chore for friends and neighbors in return for a piece of the action. As things turned out, she made quite a bit of money doing it.

What You Can Earn. To earn money in this business, you undertake to run the sale for someone else, and then take a percentage of the total proceeds. It's not unusual to charge 10 to 15 percent of the gross receipts for such assistance, and to be given first crack at the merchandise left over, to boot!

A garage sale can gross as much as $300, which means that you can net at least $45 not counting the value of the merchandise you go home with. Once you become expert at handling all the details, you can put on several during the same day.

Obviously, you need not be present during the entire sale. Most of your work is done the day before. Your client, the homeowner with the accumulation, handles most of the selling job. You get paid for organizing the stuff, pricing it, and promoting the sale.

HOW TO BUILD YOUR WEALTH BASE

Here's What You Need. You will need the drive to get things done—something that a lot of people lack. You will have to enjoy wearing old clothes and rooting about attics, cellars and garages looking for, lugging, and pricing all sorts of articles. Apart from this, very little else is required.

How to Get Started. Begin at the beginning—go to a couple of garage sales. Get a feel for the operation, and study, in particular, the prices charged for the most common items usually put up for sale. Next, you'll need a practice run.

Ask a friend who is burdened with the usual clutter and offer to thin it out with a garage sale—at no cost. Have cards printed beforehand that tell of your service. You'll use these to hand out to prospects at the sale, because you will soon discover a surprising fact. You will recognize many of the faces that you saw at previous sales you attended.

Believe it or not, there is a core of followers in just about every town who avidly follow up every garage sale. These are the inveterate bargain hunters who wind up cluttering their own garages and homes with stuff they've bought. Sooner or later, they'll have to clear the stuff out and will welcome your professional help.

How to Promote. The direct method of handing out cards at sales you run is the best way to go about promoting your business.

Spread the word, also, to your friends, and ask them to recommend you to their friends. You can arrange to run sales for churches, social clubs, and other groups where all the members bring their unwanted articles and donate the proceeds to the organization.

Even if you make little money handling one of these fund-raising affairs, the exposure is good for your name and business.

Promoting the actual sale at a specific time and place is invariably done with a classified ad. Many newspapers even have headings for these columns that read, "Garage Sales" because the events are so numerous and popular. The homeowner always pays for the cost of this advertising.

Your Opportunity for Growth.   To expand this basic business, consider having a few associates who can help you run sales when too many fall on the same day. If you find it possible to supervise three sales during a Saturday, the addition of two assistants will enable you to handle a total of nine sales on that day. Even if you split the income 50-50 with your helpers, you've still made a healthy profit on the day's work.

You can also arrange with your customers to let you sell some of your own merchandise at their sales. This is the stuff you've accumulated from previous sales and it always brings you a good profit because it cost you nothing to acquire.

A good experience in this business can lead you to many other interesting byways to profit—auctioneering, antique selling, nostalgia collecting, and other related activities. As a business, it's another easy building block to add to the main job of building your Wealth Base.

THE GOOD-BUY BUSINESS

Report on Products for Profit

Your Opportunity for Profit.   When you read newspaper advertisements there is often a tendency to disbelieve what is being said.

After all, the merchants are paying for these ads to bring people into their stores to buy their products. But, if you read about the same merchandise in the editorial columns, it is often more believable, and generally "moves" a lot more merchandise.

If you have a feel for the retail business, and have a modicum of writing ability, the "Good-Buy" business is for you. Here's how it works. You go around to all the store owners and tell them that you are starting a paid editorial column in the local newspaper. That is, you plan to buy newspaper space, but will have it set up so that it appears to be an editorial feature and therefore more believable.

In the column, you will discuss, in a chatty way, what you feel are the "best buys" of the week. Actually, what you are doing is writing about the products the retailers are featuring that week. And each retailer pays you for his share of the space. In essence, you have become an authority on merchandise to the readers. Be sure to use your name and a picture. This conjures up the image of expertise that makes this ad column very successful.

What You Can Earn. Your earnings will depend on how many retailers you can sign up, and the cost of the advertising space in the paper. For example, if your local paper has a rate of 35¢ a line (there are 14 lines to the column inch) you will pay $4.90 per inch of newspaper space. As you use more space, the rate goes down. You should try to plan far enough ahead so that you can take a lot of space on a yearly contract rate to get the reduced price.

We can't quote actual figures because rates vary from paper to paper. But, assuming that you can sign up 10 stores for 2″ of space a week, you will then be using 20″ of space each week. At $4.90 an inch, your cost will be $98. You can easily sell this space to your clients at a 50% to 100% premium. After all, they are not buying ordinary advertising space. They are buying a mention in a chatty column of news that is read as a regular news feature.

HOW TO BUILD YOUR WEALTH BASE

Here's What You Need. Basically, all you need is a typewriter, or someone to type for you, and the time to sell the service and collect the "news."

How to Get Started.   Write up a sample column, using actual store names of those you plan to solicit, and mention the actual products they are selling. When you have it completed, visit each store owner and show it to him. Seeing his name "in print" is a powerful tool. Be sure to discuss the advantage of this kind of "editorial" approach. Be quick to point out that he should still run ads in the paper as well. After all, the paper could lose a lot of business if you let this get out of hand.

How to Promote.   This must be sold in person. You can follow up your sales calls with a personal letter, re-emphasizing all the advantages of your service, but it must be a person-to-person sale.

Your Opportunity for Growth.   If your column gets too big and unwieldy, you might lose customers. After all, somebody has to be at the bottom of every story, and if they are there too long, there will be complaints.

Your answer is to specialize—start a hardware column—a food column—a clothes column, etc.

GOURMET COOKING

Getting a "Taste" for Money

Your Opportunity for Profit.   Say "gourmet" cooking to the average person and he immediately thinks of a fancy menu printed in French, and impossible to read without help from a snooty waiter.

Yet, when you add that mysterious dash of your "secret" ingredient to plain, ordinary hamburger, you are engaged in a form of gourmet cooking. Gourmet cooking simply means making everyday foods taste like something special from the menu of a posh restaurant or hotel. If you like to cook, then don't overlook this potential money-maker of a business in the kitchen.

For instance, Bertha Mueller started a modest catering business serving small weddings, parties, and other social functions. As she gained confidence in her ability to please people with her cooking, she began reading gourmet cookbooks, and experimenting with the recipes. To her surprise, she found that gourmet cooking was no more difficult than most ordinary cooking, and the rewards much greater. Her catering business zoomed, to the point where she "nets" over $10,000 a year, and still has ample time for her family.

What You Can Earn.   There are two ways to make money with your pots and pans: cook for others, or show others how to cook for themselves. If you like the idea of teaching, you can offer courses in your own home. Or, you can explore the thought of offering a course at the local adult education class.

Lessons are usually given to groups of 3 to 8 people, especially if you are using your own kitchen as a classroom. For a course of 10 lessons, it is not unreasonable to charge 75 to 100 dollars, including the cost of the food consumed. If you have 8 people in your course, you can make $600 to $800 for a 10-week course that meets only once a week. Of course, if you can manage all the tasting involved in a teaching course like this, you can offer more than one course a week.

HOW TO BUILD YOUR WEALTH BASE

Here's What You Need.   You will, of course, need to know something about gourmet cooking. This is not especially difficult. You can pick up valuable pointers by taking a course offered at a school or by someone else, or by reading some of the many books available on the subject. Tell your librarian what you want, and you probably won't be able to carry all the books she can recommend.

You will also need the basic tools and utensils. These include an egg whisk, a set of top-stove saucepans, and ovenware, French knives, a spatula, measuring spoons and cup, kitchen shears, and a grater. As your ability grows, you will find yourself depending more and more on a few of these utensils. This equipment costs less than $50.

How to Get Started.   Once you get comfortable in your cooking ability, contact some of the women's groups in your area. Ask if they would like a free lecture-demonstration on gourmet cooking. Few program chairmen will turn down such an offer, and you will have taken one step closer toward building your reputation.

When you give your talk, whet your listeners' appetites figuratively and literally. Pass out loads of samples of your product— don't skimp on demonstration quantities. Everyone should be able to get a generous sample of everything you prepare during the program.

Remember this trick: tell just enough to show how easy a recipe is, but don't tell all. This will generate a lot of questions from the audience. Make a point of remembering those persons asking the most questions—they are hot prospects for your next class in cooking. It is not unlikely to sign up a class right on the spot; since everyone wanting the course is there, you can quickly agree on a convenient time and place for everyone interested.

How to Promote.   It's doubtful whether you can generate much interest from the usual advertising methods. Rather, concentrate on the lecture-demonstration route to building your classes. Also, remember to have an adequate supply of printed folders to pass out to interested parties at your lecture.

Your Opportunity for Growth.   Usually, your students will be happy to learn to cook a few dishes. However, when they plan to entertain, you can suggest they engage you as a "gourmet consultant" to assist them with more elaborate dishes.

Actually, you will use this opportunity to prepare some things you never touched upon in class. This, of course, leads to further lessons as guests comment on the food to the hostess.

Later, you might consider preparing special foods and distributing them through commercial channels. This, of course, requires a lot of equipment, capital, special permits, and professional help. But many successful, million-dollar businesses started out in just this modest fashion.

GRINDING AND SHARPENING

Edge Your Way to Success

Your Opportunity for Profit. Take a good look around the average person's home and you'll be amazed at the number of tools that depend on a sharp edge for doing their best work. There are, for example, such things as lawnmowers, saws, knives, hand tools, garden tools, and even shovels that require periodic sharpening.

Yet, this same tour around Mr. Average's home will invariably show you that he is very neglectful of keeping his tools sharp, and as a result, usually works twice as hard as he should in doing jobs around the house and yard. This is where you can profit with only a small investment in sharpening tools.

This business, which can be started with nothing more elaborate than a grinding wheel, a sharpening stone, and a few files, can be easily expanded into a small commercial shop handling the sharpening of specialty items like carbide-tipped saw blades, and other special cutting tools. Space requirements are very small, and the work can be handled easily on a spare-time basis.

What You Can Earn. Your labor should be figured out to net you near $5 an hour. If you can sharpen four saws in that time, your charge would come to $1.25 per blade. This is about right for a "wholesale" charge, because you will discover that a lot of business can be sent to you through your local hardware store dealer or building materials dealer. They will add 50 cents to a $1 to your charges in order to provide this service to their customers and make it worth their while. A retail price of $2 to $2.50 for this particular job is fair to the customer for the work done.

HOW TO BUILD YOUR WEALTH BASE

Here's What You Need. An electric grinder with several different wheels of different grits, a few files, a good combination oilstone and a chisel and plane blade sharpener will handle the majority of your sharpening requirements. Depending on how much you spend for a grinder, the above outfit should come to no more than $50. More elaborate sharpening shops can cost somewhat more.

How to Get Started.   A good way to start is to think like a potential customer for your service. Where would you go if you had a dull saw . . . a nicked lawnmower blade . . . or skates that needed sharpening? The answer is obvious—the place where you bought the items in the first place. List these places in your area and you'll be surprised at the size of the completed list. The important thing to remember is this: few of these places provide on-the-spot sharpening service. Usually it's a job they farm out to a small businessman like yourself.

How to Promote.   Call on your local "wholesale" prospects with your offer of local service, and negotiate a price for each typical item. They'll be glad to show you their retail price list they've been using to charge customers, and you can use it as a basis for establishing a "wholesale" price that will make the deal profitable for both of you.

Another avenue, of course, is your own "retail" trade. This means small, but consistent ads that can be easily found by a person when he wants something sharpened. The Yellow Pages and local classified advertising are ideal for this. At the beginning of the year, you could experiment with a simple postcard mailing to homeowners before the lawnmowing season begins.

Your Opportunity for Profit.   Once you have established yourself with some regular wholesale accounts, and have banked some money from your business, you should think about adding an automatic filing machine for saws. Your day-to-day contact with tool-using people makes it wise for you to consider expanding with a tool exchange, another business described in this book.

GYM AND LOCKER MAINTENANCE

Lock Up Your Future

Your Opportunity for Profit.   Some part-time opportunities are ideal for evening work, others for weekend; this one is just made for the person who has a lot of time off during the summer months. Summer is the time when a lot of catch-up maintenance must be done at schools. One of the easiest to do involves the repairing of lockers, resetting combination locks, and refurbishing of gym equipment.

The regular maintenance crew at school has a lot to do during the summer that can't be done during the time school is in session. Classrooms have to be painted, building repairs and remodeling chores must be taken care of, and the lawns and school grounds need attention. So, when the work load is heaviest on the regular school staff, you can offer a welcome service to help get the plant in shape for the opening sessions in September.

All you need are modest handyman skills. And, if you are a teacher with the summer off, you have an invaluable source of contacts for work at your own school and other neighboring ones.

What You Can Earn.   In the beginning, you'll probably have to work on an hourly basis. Your rate will probably be set by the prevailing wage rates for similar work. As you gain experience, and are able to estimate the time required to do a job, you should try to switch over to a flat "contract rate." You'll make more this way, since you're bound to find ways of speeding up the work yourself, or by hiring assistants to work for you at a lower hourly rate.

If materials are used in the work, they may be provided by the school, or you can supply them at cost plus an override for the work involved in ordering, storing, and delivering the materials

yourself. With enough work, you can even shop around for wholesale prices.

HOW TO BUILD YOUR WEALTH BASE

Here's What You Need.   A few simple tools are all you'll need
to take care of bent and damaged lockers. If repainting is involved, rent a small paint sprayer. Re-setting the locks might need
a special tool. Write to the manufacturer and find out. In all likelihood, the maintenance chief at the school has both tools and instructions for the particular locks used at his school.

Repair of gym equipment is not hard, either. Stuffing a gym
horse, or varnishing a set of parallel bars, needs no further mention. An awningmakers' needle and awl are handy for repairing
gym mats and other heavy materials. Because you'll be working
in the gym, be sure to wear sneakers to protect yourself and the
floor.

How to Get Started.   Visit the person responsible for buying this
service—the chief custodian, the principal, or superintendent of
schools, depending on the school in question. Do this before the
summer months arrive so your service can be planned for in addition to the regular work expected of the full-time custodians.

How to Promote.   Do a good job near home where you are well
known, and your promotion will just about take care of itself. This
is a needed service that other schools will seek, once they hear that
it is available. Use a low-key selling approach; visit neighboring
schools, and try to get your first customer to agree to give you a
reference.

Your Opportunity for Growth.   If one school needs help like
this, then you can be sure there are many more in need also.
Therefore, recruit friends, particularly if they happen to be teachers and have the time available in the summer months.

Before you know it, you can have teams of maintenance people
in the field every summer, while you handle the administration
and contact work. John Conte, an executive in a large Eastern
city, was told to slow down or his ulcer-producing job would kill
him. He started this business to keep a little busy while recuperat-

ing from an attack. Now he employs six people, is earning over $20,000 a year, and has freedom and independence as his own boss. Best of all, he also has a good part of the winter free to vacation as he pleases. The ulcer hasn't been heard of since.

HI-FI CONSULTANT

Tune In for Profits

Your Opportunity for Profit.   Music, of one kind or another, plays a large part in the lives of most people. And, with the new tape, disc and F.M. equipment it is possible to get excellent results at moderate prices.

But, simply buying a good piece of equipment doesn't necessarily mean that you will get the same results you heard in the dealer's demonstration room. A hi-fi system must consider the room in which it is placed as part of the total system. Equipment must be "sized" to the space, and careful consideration must be given to the placement of chairs, rugs, draperies, and other things. This is where you come in, if you have a liking for music, and some interest in the hobby of high-fidelity. You really won't need to know much about electronics, but you should have a good "ear" for music.

A lot of hi-fi gear is available at discount, and the stores that sell it do not offer any installation service. You, as the hi-fi consultant, carefully select the gear best suited to the room in which it is to be placed, and either plan the installation for the homeowner, or plan and do the complete installation.

What You Can Earn.   As a consultant you should charge for your time. Estimate the time you feel the whole project will take, and present it to your client as a total fee. Re-read Chapter 1 for the details on how to set your rates most profitably.

In addition to charging for your consulting time, you can also charge for the actual installation time, plus the building of cabinets, if any are required. In many cases, people are not anxious to have speakers loosely assembled around a room, and would prefer to have them as "built-ins." This can be a profitable addition to the business, but you must know what you are doing when you build a speaker enclosure. Before you touch one, you should read Cohen's *Hi-Fi Loudspeaker and Enclosures.* Published by Rider, it is available at most radio supply houses.

If you get into the designing and building of speaker enclosures, you will be offering a very professional service, and can charge substantial fees. It would not be unusual to charge $500 or $600, plus parts, for a stereo speaker installation in only one room.

HOW TO BUILD YOUR WEALTH BASE

Here's What You Need.   If you are going to be strictly a consultant, all you will need is knowledge, as we have already discussed. But, if you plan to do custom design and installation, you will need basic electrical tools to do the interconnecting: soldering iron, pliers, wire strippers, screwdrivers and a multi-meter. However, if you plan to build the cabinetry associated with a custom installation, you will need a well equipped wood-working shop. If you would like to stay in the role of a consultant, but would like to offer the full cabinetry service, find a partner with the power tools needed to build your designs.

How to Get Started.   Perhaps the best place to get leads is through the discount stores selling hi-fi gear. Offer them 10% of all referred business and you should be on your way. You might also work on a contract basis for them, and let them handle the billing.

Be sure to spread the word at local record and music shops as well.

How to Promote.   Most newspapers have a classified section entitled "radio, TV and hi-fi." Run regular ads of 2 or 3 lines in length to catch the readers when they are thinking of buying equipment. You might also consider renting the mailing list of people in your area who have bought from mail-order record clubs. Make a simple mailer to them.

Your Opportunity for Growth. This business can go many ways. You can develop it until you have a lucrative full-time business, in which you also become the dealer for the equipment you are installing, or you can branch out into other related services. If you do have the woodworking shop, you can handle furniture refinishing, cabinet making, and even the home-handy-man consultant, described in this book.

HOME HANDYMAN "HELPER" SERVICE

Build Profits Without Driving a Nail

Your Opportunity for Profit. Most homeowners have some improvement project in mind for their homes. For many, this immediately poses a dilemma. Imagine that Tom Culver wants to improve his basement by installing some paneling and a ceiling, and perhaps some built-ins. A professional remodeler gives him an estimate—$1700. This is too steep for Tom's finances at the moment.

The alternative for Tom is to do the job himself—perhaps at a cost of $400 for the materials alone. This figure is more in line with what Tom can afford. *But*—Tom is afraid of going ahead on his own simply because he has never tackled such a big job before.

"Suppose I make expensive mistakes, and ruin all the material with nothing to show for it?" he worries.

Basically, Tom *can* do the job. The simple skills he has picked up during years of home ownership will enable him to do a job he can be proud of—provided he could get the confidence to start.

This is where you come in—as the handyman "consultant" or helper to Tom to do the job himself.

In all probability, you've done the kind of jobs around your home that others admire—perhaps a basement room such as Tom is hankering for. You're probably the kind of person neighbors come to for help, and to borrow tools of one sort or another. If you're nodding "yes" to these statements as you read, then you have a marketable skill that can earn you easy money without any investment at all.

As a handyman consultant, you

- help order the right kinds and amounts of materials
- suggest alternate ways of doing the job
- help customers to get started on the job . . . showing what to do first and what to look out for
- offer general supervisory advice as the job progresses

Most homeowners are ready prospects for this kind of service because they can:

- save real money doing the job themselves
- work confidently, knowing you are available to answer questions or to help over the rough spots
- enjoy all the prestige from being able to say they did all the work themselves

For this help, our friend Tom would gladly pay $100, bringing his total investment in his project to $500. This figure is still a lot lower than the original $1700 estimate and the $100 you get as a "consultant" represents only a few hours work on your part.

What You Can Earn.   There is only one thing you have to sell in this business and that is your time. Go back to the first chapter which gives some suggestions on putting a value on your time and use the hourly rate you've set as your goal to give an estimate on the job.

Be business-like. Tell your prospect the number of hours you estimate he will need of your time and quote a firm figure. Any time over the estimate, at the request of the customer, will be additional at an agreed-upon hourly rate. As a rough rule of thumb, your total charges should come to between 15% and 25% of the total cost of the materials for the average job.

HOW TO BUILD YOUR WEALTH BASE

Here's What You Need. Obviously, you'll need some basic handyman know-how. But don't stop there. Decide to spend a few hours a week improving your knowledge by reading some of the many handyman and building books and magazines that are available. *Family Handyman* is especially good for keeping up-to-date on new materials and how to make use of them.

How to Get Started. Once you've decided to start, let the word around the neighborhood that you're in business. Chances are some neighbor has a job he's been putting off, or knows someone else in the same spot looking for help. One or two jobs done, and then word-of-mouth takes over fast.

How to Promote. Use the classified ads—regularly. Also try to get the editor of the local paper to do a feature on your service. This is the kind of human interest copy that newspaper editors like to run.

Another way to promote, and which won't cost you a cent, is to ask the local building materials dealer or lumber yard to carry a little poster in their window or at the counter. In return for help like this, you can steer quite a bit of business their way, and the dealers should jump at the chance of helping you.

Your Opportunity for Growth. You can earn as much as you want by working more and more hours, and by gradually upping your hourly rate. However, there is a limit to your earning capacity when you work by yourself. The next step is to add others to your "staff" and to use them as helpers on the job. Your job will become purely administrative and your profits will multiply.

You can also add other related businesses to this operation— camper maintenance and repair, antique restoration, and others.

HOME INSPECTION SERVICE FOR PROSPECTIVE BUYERS

You Sell Peace of Mind

Your Opportunity for Profit. Most people buy a home once or twice in a lifetime and it represents the biggest single outlay of money for which they will ever obligate themselves. Yet, most people spend more time shopping for clothes, cars, or appliances. Few people know what to look for in a house beyond counting the rooms, examining the neighborhood, and checking only the most obvious flaws in a house. As a result, most homes are bought with only a fragmentary knowledge of what to expect in the way of problems, what can be done to improve features, and what it might cost to adapt or remodel some existing details.

If you're fairly knowledgeable about homes and homebuilding, then you can sell your knowledge in a dignified and valuable service for prospective homeowners.

For a set fee, you examine a house from top to bottom and submit a written report of your findings. You're an objective outsider who points out potential furnace problems, or you see that the wiring is inadequate for modern appliances and say so in your report. Good features are reported, too. The basic soundness of design and construction, the value-holding history of the neighborhood, and so on, are the kind of things that will go in your report.

This report is sold to prospective buyers. When you consider the amount of money at stake, a potential homeowner will look upon your fee as a worthwhile form of insurance against making a decision he will later regret.

What You Can Earn. An average house will require a couple of hours of your time, for which you can charge up to $50. A report on a large, old house with a lot of problems is easily worth twice that amount.

While you can earn a fair amount of money in this business

alone, it is particularly suitable as an addition to other businesses of a similar nature described in this book: home repair consultant, builders' clean-up service, and home handyman helper service. Put together as a complete service for both builder and home-owner, and you have the makings of a business that can earn you $10,000 a year—and this without any investment in tools or equipment.

HOW TO BUILD YOUR WEALTH BASE

Here's What You Need.   As in the businesses suggested above, you will need little more than some basic home handyman know-how. Keep up to date by reading handyman magazines for suggestions about solving problems with new methods and materials that are constantly being introduced.

How to Get Started.   Your customers will be prospective home-owners. The way to start is to do everything to publicize the advantages of your service to this group of people. Your first lead might come from a friend who is selling his home and recommends your service to people who are potential buyers for his home. Remember—there is nothing wrong with selling the same report to more than one buyer.

How to Promote.   Small ads on the real estate pages of your newspaper are one of the best ways of publicizing your service. It is here where people are looking for homes and where you will find the most likely prospects for your service.

Introduce yourself and your service to the various realtors in town. Many times a report from you will clinch a sale for them, so they are usually willing to suggest your service to buyers who may be on the fence.

Your Opportunity for Growth.   As business increases, simply add "experts" to your staff on a part-time basis. If you can find associates who are competent in electrical and mechanical engineering, you can expand your service to include the inspection of small factories, plants, and other business buildings.

HOME REPAIR CONSULTANT

Get Paid for Leaving Your Tools at Home

Your Opportunity for Profit. If you consider yourself fairly handy around the house and yard . . . if you find that neighbors and friends ask you for advice on a wide variety of fix-it subjects —then you have the background needed to make money as a "home-repair consultant."

You are paid simply for giving advice on how to solve some problem a homeowner may be troubled with. For example:

Herb Foster is an "all-thumbs" homeowner. One day he notices a large damp spot in the corner of his basement. In his amateurish way, he can spend a lot of time and money trying to solve this "leak" with various types of basement wall coatings. Yet, Herb would be grateful if a knowledgeable person such as yourself could pinpoint the real cause of his problem—a downspout that is letting the water collect around the foundation.

What You Can Earn. This is essentially a service business in which you will use no materials. Your charges merely reflect the amount of time you spend on the job examining the problem and suggesting a solution.

Remember—your job is important to the homeowner in saving him time and money. Therefore, don't feel that your advice should be given away for next to nothing. Twenty dollars for an hour's work is not unreasonable if you can help the homeowner save $50 or $100 on needless work.

HOW TO BUILD YOUR WEALTH BASE

Here's What You Need. Your practical experience, plus some reference materials, are all you need to get started in this business. In particular, there are any number of books dealing with a variety of home repair problems that will get you out of any "tough" spot that you might find yourself in.

How to Get Started. Get to know the trusted and reliable repairmen in your neighborhood. Once you diagnose a problem for a homeowner, chances are he will ask you to recommend someone to do the work. You can pick up additional commissions from these tradespeople since you'll be steering more business their way.

How to Promote. The ideal promotion for this type of business is word-of-mouth. Your business depends on customers being impressed with your help and genuinely convinced that you've saved them money. If one satisfied homeowner begins spreading the word about how you helped him, you've gone a long way toward building a reputation and a business that will grow.

Normally, people don't know that a business such as yours exists. Another very helpful piece of promotion is some advertising specialty item that will keep your name and phone number handy in a potential customer's home. An imprinted calendar, memo pad, or similar item is an ideal giveaway since it is low in cost and has a relatively long "lifetime" around the house.

Imprinted ball-point pens are very inexpensive and you might consider carrying them with you on the job. Leave one each time you visit a home as a reminder for calling you the next time help is needed.

Your Opportunity for Growth. Apart from the normal growth associated with increased calls, you can think of eventually becoming a contractor supplying all the repair services that you will be recommending to your clients.

In other words, you keep up the consulting work and building up your business. But now, the actual workmen—the carpenters, plumbers, electricians, and others work for you as independent subcontractors. You charge the homeowner a price that includes not only your own fee, but that of the repairman also. This is a particularly desirable business from your customer's point of view.

Instead of dealing with a number of people whenever something has to be done around the house—the homeowner has a single source of maintenance and repair services. One telephone call can solve any problem . . . get any job done. At this stage, the business can be as profitable as that enjoyed by many big-time builders and contractors.

HOME SECURITY SERVICE

Profit from Protection

Your Opportunity for Profit. Most people are concerned about leaving their homes for more than a day or two without some form of protection. Of course, the local police will always cooperate with a homeowner by putting his home on the "watch list." But, during peak vacation periods, this is an extra burden on the police with heavy work schedules. Then, too, the police don't enter a citizen's home. They simply send a cruiser through the neighborhood for occasional checks, and test the doors and windows for signs of entry.

The enterprising part-timer can capitalize on this need for protection, and offer a genuine home-security service, supplementing that of the local police.

The value of your service is this: there is no substitute for real activity in and around a house to change a would-be burglar's mind. You visit your client's home at different times during the day and evening, turn on lights, open and close garage doors, and give every sign of someone at home. Any burglar "casing" houses will eliminate this one from his list.

What You Can Earn. When you consider that the average burglar alarm system for a private home may run into many hundreds of dollars, you can offer real value to a homeowner needing occasional protection by charging $5 a visit. All you need do is spend a half hour or so about the house. If these visits are made during the evening, there is absolutely no conflict with your regular job.

You can charge your customers for additional services that you can easily perform during your security visits. Checking boilers and heating system, watering plants, taking in mail, mowing lawns, and a host of additional duties can be performed for extra pay.

HOW TO BUILD YOUR WEALTH BASE

Here's What You Need.   This is another business that requires nothing more than your time. The security rounds are usually made in the evening during which you turn lights on and off in various rooms. You can also set timers to turn lights off at different times to give the appearance of activity.

If your customers don't own timers that control lights, you can get several and rent them for a small charge. In time, you will own the timers and make a profit each time you plug one in.

How to Get Started.   Your best customers, at least in the beginning, will be your immediate neighbors. Don't be shy about asking money for this service; they will offer to pay you even before you ask, if you have made it known in advance that you're setting yourself up in the security business.

Remember—your service is the only one that gives the appearance of a house actually being lived in, and explain it as such. Also when you start, make sure you tell the police of your service and whose homes you are protecting. Give them a schedule of your rounds so *you* will not be mistaken for a burglar.

How to Promote.   Because your neighbors will be your first customers, it will cost you nothing to promote this service. Simply tell them what you are doing and ask them to keep you in mind when they plan a trip. Start in the early Spring to give yourself a head-start on the vacation business.

Word-of-mouth advertising will keep getting you customers, but you might try speeding up the process by sending a simple postcard mailing to a small group of likely prospects. Your best prospects will be people with larger homes. They usually have more to protect and are willing to spend the money for the peace of mind your service will bring them.

Your Opportunity for Growth.   This is the kind of business that can grow faster than you'd expect, often leaving you too busy to handle new clients. Be ready to prepare for this in advance. Recruit friends that you can trust implicitly—those who will work with you and for you. Have them do the actual job of home watching while you handle the customer contact work.

IMPORTANT: This is strictly a watch service. *Do not, under any circumstances, carry any kind of weapon.* If a house on your route has been entered, don't touch a thing. Call the police immediately. Be sure to check with your insurance man beforehand on the possibility of carrying liability insurance for your own protection, and also being bonded for the protection of your clients.

While you are "watching" houses, there is nothing to prevent you from making some needed repairs. Be sure to tell your clients that you can take care of lawns, build patios, and install hi-fi systems, if you choose to expand in these directions.

HOME WEAVING

Turn Your Shuttle to a "Profit Express"

Your Opportunity for Profit.   Home weaving is one of the most fascinating—and profitable—of home-craft enterprises. Even with a small loom, your output can be large and impressive. More important, it is quite easy and quick to learn the craft.

Edna Wilson lived in a small resort community, where she spent her summers as a waitress in a pleasant little restaurant. To pass away the gray winter months, she began with one of the simplest of weaving devices, the Easiweave frame. This is a simple, hand-held frame, which in itself can produce beautiful pieces. Before the first winter was over she had gone thru a Fellowcrafters loom and was on her way to being a skilled artisan on a very intricate two-harness treadle loom.

By the time the summer season rolled around, Edna had become an accomplished weaver and had much to sell to the tourists in her own little shop by the ferry slip. The following year, in addition to her summer retail trade, she began selling her woven products by mail and turned the gray winters into happy, profitable months.

What You Can Earn. The output of a loom is a flat piece of cloth, and unless you plan to convert it into shaped clothes—sweaters, hats, etc.—you should plan to sell simple things that have the beauty of the weave as their main selling feature. This means scarves, shawls, and finished cloth for others to convert.

You might consider, however, making ties. They are easily made, and do not require a lot of time and effort. Your prices for these products will have to depend on the local market conditions —both the production products available in retail stores and that produced by the local weavers, if any. The authors have seen hand woven scarves selling for over $30. This may seem a lot, considering most retail stores carry scarves costing between $5 and $10. But, remember, you are selling a hand-crafted product, and the cost is entirely justified.

If you sell thru the mail, remember this important fact: You should get back at least $3 for every dollar you spend in advertising. Be sure to read the chapter on advertising carefully for the details of this formula.

HOW TO BUILD YOUR WEALTH BASE

Here's What You Need. Essentially, you will need the interest, the time, and a simple loom. Start with Easiweave and then progress to whatever compound loom best suits your needs. One of the best books for the beginner is entitled *Hand Loom Weaving for Amateurs*, written by Kate Van Cleve. Many adult schools give evening courses in weaving.

How to Get Started. Whether you live in a resort town, or a town that has never seen a tourist, the weaving business is always profitable. Start by finding several retail stores that will carry your output on a consignment basis. Also, consider local fairs, and handicraft shows as a source of exposure and sale.

How to Promote.   To promote local sales, make up some samples, and try to have shopkeepers display them on a "per-order" basis, or if you have a good stock, on consignment.

Once you've acquired some "risk capital" from this home business, try some mail-order ads in appropriate magazines. A later chapter on advertising carries information on making money through the mail.

Your Opportunity for Growth.   Your best bet for growth is through the mail. Handicraft products, such as weaving, can be sold this way because your ad reaches thousands of prospects each month. This is much more exposure than you could ever get through a local promotion. You might also consider the tie making business discussed elsewhere in this book, as a perfect "tie-in."

A great deal of helpful information on mail-order selling regularly appears in *The Franklin Letter*. Published monthly, a one-year subscription is available for $18. Write to James Franklin Associates, Box 95, Demarest, New Jersey 07627.

INCOME TAX PREPARATION

Uncle Sam Isn't the Only One Who Collects

Your Opportunity for Profit.   Most people don't realize that it isn't necessary to be a graduate accountant, CPA, or other highly-trained professional in order to make a good deal of money preparing income tax returns. Large corporations, wealthy individuals, and other taxpayers with complex forms to fill out will, of course, go to accounting firms specializing in this work. But, 90% of all the people who file tax returns each year have little or no need for such high-powered service.

These millions of taxpayers need the assistance of someone who has invested a modest amount of time making himself familiar with current tax regulations, and who can fill out a tax form. Most people dread even the simplest computation involved in the preparation of a tax return and are willing to pay someone, like yourself, to do the "drudge" work for them. Actually, the work is drudgery only when you don't know what to do. Once the instructions of filling in a tax form have been mastered, the work becomes enjoyable . . . and profitable.

What You Can Earn.   Right at the beginning you must realize that this business is seasonal. Most of your money will be made in about three months. Working hard these few months does have its advantages, though. You have a lot of time during the rest of the year to pursue other activities—and the money to do it!

As an independent tax preparer, you can average $10 to $20 an hour for your time in preparing tax returns. You can get in 400 to 600 hours of spare-time work during the busy tax season, so you can see how much it is possible to earn. Best of all, the business doesn't require an office.

HOW TO BUILD YOUR WEALTH BASE

Here's What You Need.   This business demands a liking for numbers and working with rules. If you enjoy playing cards and other games, the chances are that you have the kind of "numbers" background that is valuable in this work. The only equipment you will need are some pencils and scratch pads. After you've made some money on your first few returns, you can consider investing in a small adding machine or calculator to save time and to insure accuracy.

How to Get Started.   Some time before the tax season begins, you should begin "boning up" on current tax regulations and studying filled-in sample forms to see how the various returns are made, and how the various computations are performed. The U.S. Government has instruction booklets available that will help enormously. Better still, a comprehensive tax course—one that is updated with the latest rulings and regulations—is your best bet. One of the best we know of is the FEDERAL TAX COURSE, available from Prentice-Hall, Englewood Cliffs, New Jersey 07632.

How to Promote.   Unlike other professionals—doctors, lawyers, CPA's and the like—*you* can advertise your service as a tax preparer. Most of your logical clients will be small businessmen, neighborhood proprietors, and individuals who need relatively simple tax preparation help. Basically, you reach them two ways:

- by a dignified direct-mail campaign several months before tax deadlines arrive
- and by use of consistent, small space advertising in your local newspaper during this same period

Your first few clients won't cost you anything to get. The first ones to ask for help will be your friends, relatives and other acquaintances. You should be alert to use your membership in various religious, civic, fraternal and social organizations as a means of getting business. With these relatively easy clients assured, you will soon have enough money to invest in advertising.

Your Opportunity for Growth.   In the beginning, your main concern will be getting as many clients as you can handle comfortably during the tax season. This is the first stage of growth and it comes rather quickly for a go-getter in this business. Once your time is fully committed, growth can come in two other ways:

- as your experience grows, you can do more work in less time, and still charge the same for the average tax return.
- you can break in an assistant to handle the overflow. This is an ideal situation to bring in your spouse as a partner.

Another area of growth not to be neglected is the preparation of state tax returns. Today, the majority of states have income tax laws and returns must be filed.

INDUSTRIAL BOOKSELLER

Your "Books" Will Show Nice Profits

Your Opportunity for Profit. Making money as a bookseller is nothing new. Suggest this as a business and everyone immediately thinks of a bookshop loaded with books, with all the headaches of running a retail store—a big investment in stock, long hours, pilferage, employee problems, and so on. Yet, it is entirely possible to run a profitable bookselling operation with none of these drawbacks. You don't need a store loaded with expensive inventory; you can work at your own hours, and you deal with only large-volume buyers. The secret—specialize as an industrial bookseller.

What You Can Earn. Ben Gordon was a chemist working full-time for a large company. He wasn't exactly starving in his job, but he was pretty well lost in the lab as far as real advancement or big money opportunities might go. One day, he found himself needing some specialized information and he thought he might find what he needed in a book.

His town library had no up-to-date books in highly technical areas . . . the local bookstore stocked "light popular" stuff only, and the gum-chewing teenager that tended the cash register didn't know how to find a book on polymer chemistry if her life depended on it. In desperation, Ben wrote to a number of technical publishers.

In a short time, he had answers from a number of them. Several sent brochures describing books both in the area he was interested in, and in related areas. He never knew such a variety of titles existed. He soon ordered, *at company expense,* a total of $128 worth of reference books.

Ben soon realized a *need* similar to his existed in every company, and he set out to fill them. Without too much trouble, he set himself up as an industrial bookdealer. His first clients were companies in the immediate area. Soon he started solicitations by mail. Within two years, his client list had grown to such length that he had a full-time job running a business that grossed over a quarter of a million dollars. To this day, no one has ever come in from the street to buy a book from him. The reason is simple—he has no store. All his operations are carried out from a loft in a low-rent district of town.

HOW TO BUILD YOUR WEALTH BASE

Here's What You Need. The most important ingredient for success in this business is curiosity. You should be interested to learn about various topics so you won't be frightened by technical terms. If you have some technical background, or an interest in science, so much the better.

How to Get Started. Even the smallest town library has a list of publishers, most likely in the latest copy of *The Literary Market-place.* Write to every technical and professional book publisher and ask for three things:

1. their latest catalog
2. your name to be put on their mailing lists
3. what minimum requirements you must meet to qualify as a dealer.

Publishers are anxious to expand the sales of their books and will cooperate to a surprising degree with any serious minded person who wants to get into the book business. If you have any credit reputation at all, you'll be shipped books on open account up to a certain limit.

How to Promote. In the beginning, call on every likely prospect in person. This means company librarians, chief engineers, purchasing agents, and owners of companies. They probably have a haphazard ordering system for books. You can offer them several powerful advantages:

1. Instead of dealing with a number of publishers and writing several purchase orders a week, the company can save money by ordering *all* their books through you on a single purchase order.
2. You will keep them up to date on a "standing-order" basis. If you ship them a book they can't use, neither you nor your client stand to lose any money—the books are 100 percent returnable to the publishers.

3. You can offer a discount (like 10 percent) in return for all their business.

This combination of advantages to a company is impossible to beat. Later, you can solicit companies by mail with the same offer. A list of company libraries is readily available from list brokers or the Special Libraries Association.

Your Opportunity for Growth.   This is a real "sleeper" business as far as opportunity goes. Be prepared for rapid growth, particularly if you get some clients that are in a growth technology, or happen to hit a few big contracts. Just be wary of one thing. Stock as few books as possible so you don't tie up capital in stock on your shelves. Develop efficient ordering procedures with the various publishers and send them orders as you get orders.

INDUSTRIAL CATERER

No Matter How You Slice It, You Make Money

Your Opportunity for Profit.   Everywhere you turn, new industrial parks are popping up. The people who work in the factories often have no place in which to buy food, and would welcome a "chuck wagon on wheels." This is an easy business to start, and one which you can test without a large investment.

Louis Albert worked at a nearby factory, and found that the nearest diner was always crowded, and it charged high prices. He began taking orders from his friends at the plant the night before for their next day's lunch. That night, he and his wife prepared the sandwiches, sealed them in plastic bags and stored them in the refrigerator. The next day, he took them into work with him, and distributed them at lunch time . . . for a handsome profit.

What You Can Earn.   This is the kind of business which can net you just about whatever you want. If you plan to continue it as a spare-time business, it can be a fine source of money. If, however, you would like to expand it to a full industrial catering service, it is easily done. For this reason, it is almost impossible to tell you what you can make.

But, let's take Louis' case. He decided to remain as a part-time caterer to supplement his wages at the factory. After a few months, he had over 40 people ordering food from him. He found that he averaged 60¢ profit on each sale, for a total of about $24 a day. His five day lunch hour business netted him a tidy $120 a week; which was just about what he earned in his regular factory job. Of course, he worked hard evenings, but it was well worth it.

HOW TO BUILD YOUR WEALTH BASE

Here's What You Need.   You really need nothing to start in this business. Even if you don't have a place to prepare the sandwiches, you can still get started. You can have a diner prepare them for you—at a wholesale price—and you mark them up to competitive retail prices and pocket the profits.

You do need access to a large group of people in need of lunch. That's all.

How to Get Started.   Visit all the factories in an area that you feel you can service comfortably, if you are not planning to start at your own plant. Check to see if they have a cafeteria, or a nearby diner. Even though many will have one or the other, they still represent a source of income. People are often dissatisfied with their present source of lunch, and if you can offer a "home" prepared lunch at a competitive price, you've got it made.

Be sure to check with a plant official before you begin soliciting. The personnel director is often the person who can get you started by recommending your service to the employees. And be sure to check to see if you will need a food vendor's license from the board of health.

How to Promote.   The best way to promote this business is to have small signs printed and distribute them liberally all over the plants you wish to service. Be sure to announce the time you will visit the plant, and have it coincide with the beginning of the lunch break. At this point, you probably will not be taking orders the night before, but be selling sandwiches and drinks from a stock, so a simple menu, also posted on the bulletin boards would help.

Your Opportunity for Growth. As we mentioned, this business can grow to just about any size you want, and it can also be a good source of steady, part-time income. Others who have started an industrial catering service have gone on to add trucks with cooking facilities, and even gotten into the installation of fast-food machines at the more remote plants in their area.

INTERIOR DECORATING

Here's How to Make a "Pretty" Profit

Your Opportunity for Profit. When Helen Farnsworth took a part-time job selling paint and wallpaper at a local store, she never realized that this experience, plus a few spare-time hours of reading would change her whole life. As her customers asked for advice, she realized the importance of this responsibility, and became increasingly expert in the field of interior decorating. She soon had top sales in the store, and then left to open her own interior decorating studio.

The role of the decorator is to bring out the likes of the client in terms of their home design scheme. Many decorators work as freelancers, and others are employed by home furnishing retailers. Either way, there is a lot of money to be made by anyone with a flair for making a room look interesting.

What You Can Earn. As we mentioned, you can work as a freelancer, or as an employee of a store, but it is also possible to combine the advantages of both approaches—that is, by having your own practice, and also working as a consultant to a smaller store with no full-time decorating staff.

Working for a salary, many decorators earn in excess of $20,000 a year. The free-lancer can often top this, or work at it to suit his individual needs. In any case, you should figure your time on an hourly basis, but quote a total figure to your clients. When you have gained some stature, you can easily figure your time at a minimum of $10 an hour. The figure, of course, varies from one part of the country to another.

In the larger metropolitan centers, higher rates are often possible. In outlying areas, where the interest in such a service is light, your rates would have to be proportionately lower. Because this is a highly personalized service, we hesitate to specify figures. We feel that the safest bet is to pretend you are in need of a decorator and get several estimates. This way you will have a good idea of the range of charges for various style approaches.

HOW TO BUILD YOUR WEALTH BASE

Here's What You Need.   More than anything else, you will have to like this kind of work, and have some feel for design. A knowledge of wood finishes, fabrics, furniture styles, and a good color sense are a must. A good source of training in this field is available from the Chicago School of Interior Decorating, located at 835 Diversey Parkway, Chicago, Illinois 60614.

How to Get Started.   Unless you already have some experience or training, try to get a sales job in a drapery shop, furniture store, or any businesses related to home furnishings. Once you get the feel of it, and have done some reading, try your hand at decorating a room in your home. You can make this your "show-room" and invite potential customers to view your work. Offer to help a few friends—primarily for the recommendations they will give you after the work is done.

How to Promote.   When you have a few successful rooms to your credit, and you feel confident, run a few small ads in the classified pages of your local newspaper. Be sure to get a "guest spot" as a speaker at the local women's club meeting. The question-and-answer period after your talk will give you all the clues you'll need as to who is in need of your professional assistance. You should also seek out some "consulting" assignments with the smaller home furnishing stores in your area who cannot afford a full time decorator.

Your Opportunity for Growth.   As word of your talent spreads, you will receive larger commissions for bigger homes. This is money in the bank, but you should give serious consideration to commercial work—office decoration. There is a lot of money to be made, and if you can tie in with an architect, you will never have to make another sales call.

You should also give some thought to these other related businesses discussed in this book: custom lamp making, chair caning, custom framing, and antique refinishing.

INVENTORY SERVICE FOR BUSINESS

Take Stock of Your Profits

Your Opportunity for Profit.   Every retail business selling products must take an inventory of its goods at periodic intervals. Good business management demands it; and even if a business owner felt he could do without this regular counting of stock, today's tax laws force him to do it. This is where you come in and profit mightily—and with *zero* investment!

Since inventory taking is performed a few times a year at most, few businesses can afford a full-time person or staff for just this job. Invariably, a businessman is forced into expensive overtime with his regular help, or he must call in a professional inventory service and pay them as much, or more, to get the job done. This businessman will literally jump at the opportunity of getting this irksome job done if you show him how to do it at the absolute minimum wage (or even lower!) and build priceless goodwill in the community to boot. Here's how it's done.

The answer is "volunteer" help. Yes, volunteer help for a regular, profit-making enterprise. There are scores of people in every town who will turn down a fairly generous hourly wage (because they really don't need the money), but will jump at the chance to work free if they know their labors are going to help some worthy cause.

Elaine Stein, who lived in a suburb of a big city, saw the opportunity to help her local library association in just this fashion. Located in a nearby shopping center were several branches of big-city stores—retail chains that had a need for regular, reliable, and low-cost inventory service. She approached them with the following offer: she would provide as many volunteer inventory takers as the store might need. Since they would be volunteers, the store would pay no "wages," and hence be relieved of a lot of payroll headaches.

The hours these volunteers worked were carefully recorded by a store supervisor. And, when the job was done, the store simply made out a check to the library as a "donation." The library got a substantial donation; the store got the job done at low cost, and built goodwill which is impossible to buy; volunteers doing the work were delighted to work free, knowing their efforts earned money for their favorite charity. And Elaine earned welcome cash, averaging $300 monthly.

What You Can Earn.   There are various ways you can profit in this business. The simplest is merely to have the store agree to pay you an "over-riding" commission on the hours worked by the "volunteers." Your job in this service is to line up the volunteers, keep an up-to-date list of people available and the times they have free, and to make sure that the right number of people show up at the store at inventory time. Although your volunteers work free, you should have no qualms about charging for your organizing work in putting together the inventory teams.

A typical money example might be as follows: you provide ten people to a department store for one evening and each person works four hours. That's forty man hours. The store pays for these hours in the form of a "donation" of $1.50 a man-hour, or $60 to the designated charity. You add on a 25% override, or $15 to the cost. The total cost to the store is $75—a bargain by any measure (overtime or outside help could easily cost $5 an hour or a total of $200). And you don't even have to appear at the inventory! All you do is provide the people who do the work. They are supervised by regular store supervisors.

HOW TO BUILD YOUR WEALTH BASE

Here's What You Need.   You should have access to a pool of volunteers and some worthy organizations that people are willing to work for. In a typical town this presents no problem—every church, library, boy scout, veterans group, or other organization has a following of people ready to help.

How to Get Started.   Starting is simplicity itself. Phone the manager of a local store and ask for an appointment to see him. Tell him you have a plan guaranteed to cut his inventory cost drastically, and he will see you *fast.*

How to Promote.   Selling the plan is easy, too. Describe it as above and you will probably be given an assignment right on the spot. Then, get home and on the phone. In a very short time your volunteers will be lined up and you've earned your commission— as much as $15 for an hour's work.

Your Opportunity for Growth.   Your growth and profits will be limited by the number of hours you want to work in selling this plan to various stores and businesses. To expand, get in touch with charitable organizations in outlying towns for more "volunteers." Before you know it, you can have a substantial part of the inventory business of a fairly large trading area. Most important, this clean profit will continue to come in, good times and bad, and you can handle it all, scarcely ever leaving your home or phone.

LAMP MAKING

Turn On a Bright Profit

Your Opportunity for Profit.   Mr. and Mrs. Louis Geller discovered an unusual old bottle in an antique shop on Cape Cod. Now that she has it home, Mrs. Geller thinks it would make a perfect lamp.

Unless Mr. Geller happens to have a special drill, patience, and some knowledge of lamp parts, Mrs. Geller's thoughts will remain wishful thinking. However, if you ran this custom lamp business, Mrs. Geller could have her lamp, and you could make a good profit.

Very little skill is needed to transform articles into lamps. The lamp parts are all standard and easily available. At most, you might have to add a simple wooden base or support to complete the lamp.

What You Can Earn.   Each assignment you get is different. One time it might be a bottle . . . another time it could be a coffee grinder. Even old flint-locks have been turned into floor lamps. For a person who enjoys working leisurely with his hands, this business is:

- interesting, creative, and seldom tiring
- well-paying for the time you spend
- impossible to mass-produce at a cheap price

Generally, you will estimate each job individually. After a bit of experience, you can judge how much time will be needed for any job. Charge for the estimated hours, plus the cost of your materials, and an allowance for your overhead.

If a woman brings you an old coffee grinder for transformation, a charge of $20 to $35 is quite reasonable. This does not include the shade.

HOW TO BUILD YOUR WEALTH BASE

Here's What You Need. You won't need many tools for this business. However, a small electric drill is a must. Many times you will need to drill holes in metal and glass and a hand drill is simply impractical. Ask your local hardware dealer to give you the proper speed drills for metal, and the special drill bit for drilling holes in glass.

Lamp parts, too, are readily available in hardware stores. Regardless of the article being converted into a lamp, all you'll be doing is adding some sturdy means of holding a socket to the item. The socket holds the bulb and the bulb holds the shade. It's that simple.

How to Get Started. Spend an hour or two shopping around a large, well-stocked lamp shop. See how the various standard lamp parts are adapted to make interesting lamps. The next step is to turn some items into lamps that can be used as samples to show potential customers what can be done . . . and what you can do.

How to Promote. Our old standbys serve well here—classified ads and yellow page advertising. Word-of-mouth advertising is invaluable, too. Do a job that pleases a woman, and, before you know it, members of her clubs and social groups will start calling.

Another important source of business not to be overlooked is the local antique dealer. Let him know that you can transform objects into lamps. A browser in his shop might be only half interested in some object, but will buy it immediately if she is told that a reliable artisan can make the object into a lamp that will be treasured as a conversation piece in her living room.

Your Opportunity for Growth. This business can provide a few hours of pleasant, profitable work a month, or it can become a very lucrative full-time business. It depends on how much time you are willing to devote to it, and the effort you expend in promoting your service.

As an additional source of money, you might buy items yourself for transformation and sell them as ready-made lamps. This, of course, would require some showroom space. Make a deal with the antique dealer to handle these items on consignment.

LANDSCAPE PLANNING

Plant Your Own "Money" Tree

Your Opportunity for Profit.   Landscape architecture is a recognized profession that requires years of schooling. Yet, the basics of *landscape planning* can be acquired by anyone interested in this enjoyable work without long years of study. If you enjoy planning and maintaining the grounds around your own home, then you are well ahead on the road toward a business that can be very rewarding, both personally and financially.

There is no lack of material from which you can learn. One of the best sources is the United States Government. Write to the Superintendent of Documents, Government Printing Office, Washington, D.C. and ask for a listing of books and pamphlets covering gardening in your area of the country. You'll be amazed at all the free and low-cost information that is available from this source.

Courses are many times available at local adult education schools, at extension divisions of state universities, and by mail. **What You Can Earn.**   Some people earn handsome, five-figure incomes from the practice of landscape design. What you can earn varies greatly depending on your skill and the amount of work you do. Here are some of the interesting and exciting things you do to earn substantial fees in this business:

- you visit the home of your client and make simple measurements and sketches of his property
- you discuss with your client his needs and desires. Does he want planting or play areas? Privacy or a clean sweep of lawn? And so on.
- you make a simple sketch of your client's property on a large sheet of graph paper. On this you indicate plants, trees, shrubs, and other landscape elements that you would recommend. You will even suggest such things as walks, terraces, and fencing when desirable.
- you present this plan to your client. Minor changes are usu-

ally made at this point to accommodate some last-minute ideas the owner may have.

Once approved, the plan is turned over to the homeowner or a professional nursery contractor to do the actual work. The heaviest thing you ever lift is a pencil. A typical job, covering all the steps mentioned above, is easily worth several hundred dollars. This is a very small investment for the client to make when you consider how much he is spending for his home. A good landscaping job always adds more to the actual value of the house than the actual amount of money spent on plans and plantings. Needless to say, this is your biggest sales point to make whenever you call on a prospect.

HOW TO BUILD YOUR WEALTH BASE

Here's What You Need. Start out right away building an idea file. Clip everything of interest that can help you solve a problem later on. For example: ideas on handling an unsightly view, getting privacy on a narrow building lot, taking advantage of a sloping lot, and so on. Store these clippings in folders that will let you find them easily later on.

Build a library of reference materials, also. Books, magazines, and government publications will broaden your knowledge amazingly. If you want further help, you should investigate the reasonably priced mail-order course and landscaping kit that is available from the American Landscaping Guild, Box 95, Demarest, New Jersey 07627.

How to Get Started. Do one job free in order to gain some recognition and to have a "sample" to refer prospective clients to see. You might take a hint from Phyllis Milne who volunteered her services to the local school board which had just completed building a new school. They were delighted to get a plan at no cost to the taxpayers, and she got quite a few inquiries from the publicity it generated.

How to Promote. Cultivate the owner of your local garden shop or nursery. Their main profit comes from selling plants, so they can't afford to give extensive planning help to a customer. If you describe your business to them, they will usually be glad to recommend your service since it can mean more business for them, too.

If a builder is developing a tract of homes nearby, you have another ready market. Nicely planned landscaping should cost no more than haphazard plantings done with no imagination. Yet, the difference is great enough to make a house look larger, more expensive, and worth more than its neighbor with poor landscaping. A good landscape plan helps sell homes for a builder, and you should exploit this selling point to the fullest.

When you see a new home going up, find out the name of the owner. Usually, a nearby family knows who is building near them. Write to the new owners before they move in. Tell them of your service and refer them to jobs you may have done in the neighborhood. Suggest how much larger and elegant their new home will look if they let a professional plan the landscaping.

Your Opportunity for Growth. Your growth will come in two ways. First, you will get more and more jobs to handle as your reputation and skill increases. Second, as you become more expert, you can take on complex jobs that can bring in really big fees. At this point, you should hire the services of a free-lance draftsman to draw the actual plans, while you concentrate on the overall design and the selection of the plants.

Later on, you can also earn extra fees by supervising the actual work being done by the nursery contractor to make sure it conforms to your plans and ideas.

LEATHERCRAFT

Hand-tooled Profits

Your Opportunity for Profit. When Henry Hart returned from a tour of duty with the Navy, he went back to college, but found that his GI bill was not sufficient to support him. Casting about for part-time work, he came up with the idea of using a craft he had perfected during a 3 month tour of sea duty—custom leathercraft.

Henry bought a set of the basic tools, costing about $30, some good leather, and turned out about a half-dozen samples of wallets, pocketbooks, belts, and key cases. Armed with these samples, he made the rounds of the better men's and women's clothing and accessory shops, and was able to get several of the proprietors to display his samples, and to take orders for custom leather work.

Learning leather craft is not difficult, and it can be a source of great pleasure as well as profit.

What You Can Earn. It is all but impossible to make any money in anything but a custom operation here. But, with everything being produced on special order, by a skilled artisan such as yourself, you can charge prices that far exceed most of the better, but mass produced products. For example, when Henry was actively plying his craft, he often received over $100 to produce an intricately tooled pocketbook. Highly personalized belts and wallets have brought as much as $35 and $50 a piece.

Once you have achieved some proficiency in the craft you should be able to do the design, tooling, and assembly of a large pocketbook in three or four evenings. Material cost for such a project would seldom exceed $25. The rest, obviously is ample reward for the skilled work you have mastered. Henry was able to supplement his GI Bill to the tune of approximately $4000 a year for very pleasant, part-time work.

HOW TO BUILD YOUR WEALTH BASE

Here's What You Need. There are certain basic tools that you must have: A skiving knife, several mallets of different weights, single and multiple blade punches, and, of course, the set of stippling and patterning tools. A good set of these tools should not exceed $35 or $40 in cost.

The leather is bought as needed, but don't hesitate to buy a particularly good piece on the speculation of future business. Because the prices of leather vary with the kinds of hides, and the particular market conditions, it is all but impossible to give you any costs here. But, this price is always charged off to the customer in the final price, which is based on time and materials.

How to Get Started. If you have never worked with leather, visit an arts and crafts store and buy yourself a beginners' kit. Do not invest in all the tools until you have found that you like the work.

Once you have achieved some facility, make up a number of samples, and take them to the men's and women's fashion stores. Explain to the proprietor that you can do any kind of leather work on special order, and for allowing your display in his store, you will give him a commission on every sale. Start out by offering 10%, but if necessary don't be afraid to give as much as 15% or 20%. After all, this is about the best kind of advertising you can get.

How to Promote. If you decide to go a route other than the store-commission approach, you might run small ads in the local paper, or even consider giving talks at social gatherings. Because this is an artistic kind of business, you must always have samples available to show.

Your Opportunity for Growth. Honestly, once you have reached your capacity, there is very little room for growth. If, however, you can either train or locate other talented leather workers, you can become a commission merchant, and get "off the bench" to reap bigger profits.

You might even consider other custom businesses, some of which we have discussed in this book: custom lamp making, custom framing, and even interior decorating.

MANUSCRIPT EDITING AND TYPING

Others Write a Future for You

Your Opportunity for Profit. Many people write. Some for fun, some for profit, and others out of necessity. Eventually, most of these people require good, error-free typewritten copy for submission to a publisher, to an academic committee, a technical journal, or to a business. Businessmen usually have access to trained typists in their offices. But, writers, teachers, lecturers, students and others must either laboriously type manuscripts themselves, or turn to a professional like yourself.

Typing is an ideal job to do at home. If, in addition, you have a good command of punctuation, grammar and spelling, you have the makings of a very successful manuscript editing and typing business.

Most churches and clubs often elect a secretary and expect this person to take notes, and type up the minutes. You can relieve them of this responsibility and make a tidy profit in the process. Watch the social sections of your newspaper for club elections, and contact the new secretaries immediately.

What You Can Earn. The usual way to charge is by the *finished* page. Never estimate by the number of pages submitted to you. Many times there are additions and corrections that require more time and space. For simple typing, a basic charge of 30 to 50 cents a finished page is about right. And, if the manuscript is very technical, or includes a great deal of mathematical figures, footnotes, or other symbols, you can then double or even triple the basic charge.

HOW TO BUILD YOUR WEALTH BASE

Here's What You Need. Obviously, you will need the ability to type well and accurately, and have access to a good typewriter. If you expect to do any variety of work at all, your ideal typewriter is an electric machine with typefaces that you can change to suit a particular job. A very good machine is the IBM Selectric. If you can't manage the purchase price at first, you might consider renting one with an option to buy after you've earned some money.

How to Get Started.   Once you've gotten your typewriter and a supply of paper, you are ready to go into business. One hint—make sure your workplace is pleasant and comfortable. Don't make the mistake of trying to do professional work in makeshift surroundings. Your worktable should be the right height, your lighting both adequate and glarefree, and your space free enough to enable you to spread out papers, and to collate manuscripts. A small radio tuned to an all-music station can greatly improve your output—and your working comfort.

How to Promote.   If you live in a university town, a simple business card tacked up on the students' and faculty bulletin boards will probably get you all the business you can handle. If you live away from such a facility, consider these business-getting techniques:

- go to your library and find out the names and addresses of the various writers' magazines. Consider using classified ads in them to build up a sound mail-order typing business
- let your local businessmen know of your services through personal letters. Many times, they have special projects that would overload their regular typists and would be glad to have the help you can offer.

Your Opportunity for Growth.   You can only type so fast and consequently your growth is limited. If business becomes overwhelming, and it's apt to happen during certain busy seasons, be ready with extra helpers. With a little scouting about, you can surely find other typists who would be willing to take your overflow work, on which you also make a profit.

You should plan to become a typists' "clearing house" as soon as possible. Use the services of the many "retired" secretaries who have become housewives. You're then off the keyboard and making money as a typing contractor.

MEDICAL EQUIPMENT EXCHANGE

Prescription for Profit

Your Opportunity for Profit. Charlie Larsen, while working on his regular job, fell from a wall and spent the next three months in a wheelchair. Renting a wheelchair for all this time seemed almost as expensive as buying one—which Charlie finally wound up doing. Now well, Charlie has a perfectly good wheelchair lying unused in the attic. Here's where a smart part-timer like yourself can make money running a medical equipment exchange.

Think of the many wheelchairs, walkers, crutches, and other big-ticket items that are lying about unused in people's homes long after the accident or illness has been forgotten. There is easy money in this store of equipment—money you can earn without a big investment.

What You Can Earn. There are two ways to make money in this business. You can buy this used equipment and then rent it out at a price that ultimately pays for the equipment and returns you a profit. You can try this avenue once you've accumulated some capital. In the beginning, you can act as a "broker" and invest nothing more than your time.

In most cases, you won't even have to store the equipment. You merely pick it up from the owner, and deliver it to the person renting it. It is returned directly to the owner or another renter when the person is finished with the item.

The best way to set your prices is to check with a friend who may work in a doctor's office or a drugstore. Set your prices somewhat lower than the commercial rate, and then split the fee with the owner of the equipment.

HOW TO BUILD YOUR WEALTH BASE

Here's What You Need.   You need little or nothing to start. If you don't get involved in buying the equipment, you won't need anything but some pre-printed bills on which you can invoice your customers. This is important since your charges will be a tax-deductible item for your customers.

If you eventually do get into the used equipment business, then you'll need space to store the items. This need not be an expensive store-type location. If your own garage isn't suitable, any ground-floor location in a low-rent location will serve nicely.

How to Get Started.   Begin by making an inventory of equipment lying unused in your home and the homes of your friends. Most of them will be happy to find an outlet that will enable them to recover some of their investment. To round out your "inventory" try running a few ads in the classified columns of your paper under the "wanted to rent" headings. Be specific in your wants; otherwise you'll be hounded by everyone in town who has a cane for sale.

How to Promote.   Talk to your doctor first. He can be a valuable source of tips and information. Certain doctors, such as bone specialists, usually have many more patients needing special medical equipment, than general practitioners.

Spread the word within your groups of associates—lodges, clubs, and the place where you work. Ask your wife to do the same within her group of friends. You'll be pleased with how much publicity you can get this way since everyone is sympathetic toward a person wanting to save money when sick or injured. Word gets around.

One of the best ways to promote this business is to use the technique used by large drug firms in promoting their prescription drugs—make friends with the nurses and receptionists in doctors' offices. A good way to do this is to give them some small gift that they can use in their work and which will carry a reminder of your name, service, and phone number. A desk pad or a small medical dictionary are ideal for this purpose.

Finally, remember that fraternal organizations generally have plans to help fellow members in times of sickness and distress. You might want to get in touch with the officers of your local clubs and offer reduced rates to members if the equipment is rented through the organization.

Your Opportunity for Growth.   Other than by simply expanding your territory of operations, your best bet for growth is to become a full-time dealer in new and used equipment, offering both sales and rentals. Just hope at this point there isn't another go-getter like yourself just starting out in the medical exchange business— he'll give you a run for your money.

You can add other "exchange" businesses to this—tool exchange, arts and crafts exchange, etc.

MIMEOGRAPH SERVICE

Profits in Printing

Your Opportunity for Profit.   Have you ever thought how handy it would be to have a simple way of duplicating letters, notes, instructions, or what-have you? And, how valuable it would be to be able to distribute what you have printed in some quantity? Most people have this need at one time or another, yet few people own a mimeograph machine or similar duplicating device.

Of course, for most people, owning one would be an extravagance. But, not for you if you can get all those other people to come to your with their odd jobs. These small jobs can add up, not only sufficiently to enable you to buy and maintain a good little machine, but also to turn a good profit in the bargain.

Most businesses, schools and churches have their own machines because they have frequent need for many printed copies. Yet, the opportunity does exist to earn a fair amount of money from other sources. Provided, of course, you know how to go about getting the business.

What You Can Earn. Mimeographing is fairly competitive in price and you should be guided by what larger shops charge in near-by cities. About $2 to $3 per hundred copies is about right if the customer provides his own stencil. If you have a good typewriter, you can make stencils for your customers and charge another $2 or so.

After you've paid for the machine (which can be picked up for less than $50 if you shop for a second-hand model) your only expense will be paper, ink and occasional maintenance on the machine.

HOW TO BUILD YOUR WEALTH BASE

Here's What You Need. A mimeograph machine, some supplies, and you're ready to go into business. You will need space to store a fair amount of supplies, and also room for a large, smooth table or counter. This is necessary for laying out and collating multi-page jobs. Do a few "free" jobs to get some samples that you can show to prospects.

How to Get Started. First, start with a consistent program of classified ads in your local newspaper, and later in the yellow pages of your telephone directory. You can't do much to "sell" the idea of mimeographing. Rather, your business will grow if your name can be easily found by whoever is looking for duplicating services.

Second, make a list of all the businesses and organizations in town that could possibly use mimeographing services and send them an announcement.

Restaurants are an ideal source. They change menues daily, and most would welcome a mimeographing service to lend a hand. Once you get their style down pat, they will call the copy on the phone and you simply print, deliver, and collect the money.

How to Promote. Your classified ads are like business cards— always working for you with interested prospects. Mimeo a good looking letter describing your service and send it to the people whose names appear on the list you compiled. This is a good follow-up technique to use after the post card mailing. Use these benefits to appeal to business men in particular:

- even if the business owns a mimeograph machine, it is cheaper usually to give the work to an outside service specializing in such work
- a machine which is used only once a month for price lists or sales information is not earning anything while it is idle. (You may not only pick up a job this way, you might also be able to buy a good second-hand machine with this argument.)
- a mimeo machine works best when it is used often. It's uneconomical to have to clean the machine if it's used only once and then left unused for long periods

Your Opportunity for Growth.   Your growth here will depend on how hard you want to sell and how far afield you're willing to go for business. With assistants picking up materials from a number of accounts, you can run a fairly substantial business, particularly if you get to the point of investing in sophisticated mimeograph or offset machines. And, don't forget, with a mimeograph machine you have the basic tool for turning out a "want-ad newspaper," a business described elsewhere in this book.

NEWSPAPER FREE-LANCE REPORTER

Your Name in Print Is Worth Money

Your Opportunity for Profit.   This is a neat way to make money for a person who is busy with community activities, while providing the volunteer service he or she is interested in performing. The ideal person for this business is a woman who is active in half-a-dozen organizations in and around town. Such a person usually knows what's happening, who is planning and doing what, and just about every important thing going on in town.

This describes the perfect newspaper reporter, and is exactly what we are suggesting. Most small town newspapers can't afford a really good reporter who can get around to the various meetings, affairs, and happenings that make up the bulk of small town news. If you're the type of person "in everything" then you can be the perfect eyes and ears of the local press.

What You Can Earn. Being a small town free-lance newspaper reporter, in itself, will not make you rich. But, you will get paid something for all the things you'd be doing free anyway. However, all through this book, we've been suggesting ways to build your personal Wealth Base by various means. Many of the businesses we have described can be combined with others to form a truly profitable avenue toward your wealth goal. Being a newspaper reporter can help you, or your spouse, with just about any business you can think of.

No, we are not suggesting that you use the news columns to promote yourself or your business. Rather, being a reporter, even in a small town, will immediately give you prestige, and a great deal of valuable contacts. These contacts are the ones that can make you rich in other businesses. Only your own imagination will limit how this advantage can be exploited.

HOW TO BUILD YOUR WEALTH BASE

Here's What You Need. You will need the contacts that you get in your normal community activities. Once you become a reporter, you'll gain more, naturally. You should be able to write a news story, but this does not require great writing talent. Basically, a news story simply answers the questions of What, Who, Where, When and Why.

How to Get Started. The best way to get started is to get some practice writing news stories. You can do this most simply by becoming the Publicity Chairman of one or more of the organizations you belong to and then simply sending in regular news items to the local paper. Soon you will get known at the editorial offices. The fact that you don't get paid for these stories should not prevent your getting paid for stories in the future.

How to Promote.   Once you've gotten a few of your news stories published by the paper, call on the editor and tell him you are interested in working on free-lance assignments. Chances are, he'll give you one right then and there. Small town newspapers are usually pressed for help because they can't afford full-time staff members, and part-timers who know what is needed are hard to find.

Your Opportunity for Growth.   Growth in this business will come by the contacts you make that will help your other businesses. The reporting business in itself will cover your expenses of running around after stories. You can earn some money in the reporting profession, and gain increased satisfaction, if you learn to handle a camera and can produce pictures for use with the important stories.

NEWSPAPER WHOLESALER

An "Extra" Profit for You

Your Opportunity for Profit.   How do you get your daily paper? Some people buy a copy each morning when they go to work. Others get a paper delivered by a neighborhood newspaper boy. If you think a moment about this latter case, you'll see an opportunity to make a fair amount of money, year in and year out with absolutely no risk on your part.

A typical newspaper operation works like this, particularly in a smaller town: a large area newspaper serves a number of towns. In each town, there is one or more newspaper wholesalers. The papers are delivered to these people who pay for them at wholesale rates. The various newspaper boys pick up their papers from the wholesaler and pay a somewhat higher rate. The difference in price is the wholesaler's profit.

What You Can Earn.   The beauty of this operation is the absence of risk. The newspaper boys are generally recruited by a separate department of the paper. All you do is supply them with the required number of papers they need for their routes. Working a few hours each day can typically earn you a clear $50 a week. Because the job requires working with youngsters and a certain amount of paperwork, the business is ideal for a woman who does not have the time for a regular job because of household duties.

HOW TO BUILD YOUR WEALTH BASE

Here's What You Need.   Clean, dry space is about all you need for this business. Remember a newspaper is published and delivered rain or shine. When the newspaper truck delivers the papers in bulk to you, you'll need a place to shelter them until the newspaper boys arrive to pick up their individual bundles.

How to Get Started.   Getting started here means getting yourself in the proper frame of mind to be a success in this business. You will be working with young people, and they require more follow up than adult workers. Sometimes, especially with morning papers, the papers will be delivered very early in the morning. You'll get to know what a sunrise looks like. And finally, you should have someone reliable to back you up—either a relative or a neighbor. The papers will have to be delivered to the boys, even if you're sick or on vacation.

How to Promote.   You don't promote in the usual sense here. Rather, call on the circulation manager of the larger newspapers in your county and tell him you want to be considered for any possible openings. If all the jobs are filled, you'll just have to wait until an opening occurs. Because of the turnover in this business, the opportunity may come sooner than you think.

Your Opportunity for Growth.   This business starts out at a fairly decent level and stays pretty constant. The newspaper management will usually consider setting up additional wholesalers in different areas rather than give one person a monopoly on all the papers in town.

Don't let this discourage you, however. Remember, this is a zero-investment, no-risk business that gives you a regular boost to your Wealth Base without promotion on your part.

NOSTALGIA

Making Money from Memories

Your Opportunity for Profit. Conjure up an image of some movie idol of the past in full costume on the cover of a movie fan magazine of the 30's, and you've got a good mental picture of $25 or so. Yes, back copies of certain magazines no older than this can bring as much as $300 from a serious collector. These are not oddball publications, either. They are the magazines that were popular during the period and of which millions upon millions of copies were sold weekly. In attics and garages all over the country must be piles of these forgotten treasures waiting to be found by a knowledgeable collector such as yourself.

In addition to magazines and old comic books, there is a ready and rapidly growing market for the trinkets and other memorabilia of the past few decades—Orphan Annie mugs and de-coder rings, Captain Midnight badges, souvenirs of past Worlds' Fairs, campaign buttons with pictures of long forgotten candidates, and many other items too numerous to mention.

You can make money seeking after these nostalgic pieces of the past, and selling them to collectors. The fun part of this business is that you're on a perpetual treasure hunt.

What You Can Earn.   You simply can't peg an earnings figure for this business. One lucky find can make you wealthy overnight. More likely, however, is a fair income for the time you invest looking for and selling the items you find. A big advantage with this business is that you can combine it with attic and cellar cleaning business described elsewhere in this book. If your regular work takes you into people's homes, you can keep your eyes open for items of interest while you're doing your regular work. Give yourself plenty of "money margin" on things you buy. Try to get that old "fan" magazine for a quarter or so . . . then try to get your $5 for it when you sell it to a collector.

HOW TO BUILD YOUR WEALTH BASE

Here's What You Need.   All you need is the spirit of a treasure-hunter—someone who loves to look and dig wherever he goes. This means you should be able to go up to a house where you suspect a "find" is possible, explain your reasons to the owner, and then bargain for whatever you may find of interest.

Be careful not to get stuck with a supply of plain junk. More about this later. You should also have a safe place to store your stuff. A dry cellar or garage is ideal.

How to Get Started.   Bone up on what is being collected, and what is being sold. The best way to do this is to browse shops that specialize in these items and ask a lot of questions. In smaller localities, a local antique dealer will many times handle items of this nature. There are magazines for collectors that your librarian can refer you to.

Finding your source of supply is not too hard, either. Check your neighborhood for families that have lived in the same house for many years. More than likely they have an accumulation of many years of junk in their attic that might just turn up something of value. Watch for families that are moving out of your neighborhood. This is the time people get rid of a lot of things, and will often let you have them just for the convenience of your carting the stuff away.

How to Promote.   Buyers of nostalgia have one habit in common—they are all avid readers of the "articles for sale" columns of the newspapers. This is the bargain hunters and collectors common meeting ground. Take advantage of it! Run separate ads for both your wants and for what you have for sale. It is usually smarter to run such ads for specific items rather than advertise the nature of your business. Generally, you'll get an item cheaper if the seller doesn't think he is dealing with a commercial dealer.

Take a small booth at some charity fair sponsored by a local group, and create some simple, attractive displays. If the fair is commemorating some anniversary, try to show off some articles dating from that period and you'll be amazed at the interest you'll generate.

You can also arrange to sell (and also buy) items at garage sales. Another section of this book tells you how to cash in on garage sales and you should review this material for more information.

Your Opportunity for Growth. It's possible to develop this business into a very profitable part-time activity. Real expansion can come with the opening of a shop, or by expanding into the antique business. By the time you're ready to consider this, you will surely have picked up quite a bit of knowledge on many areas of old furniture and other household articles, and this can be a good move.

OLD CLOCK REPAIR

Tick Tock Dough

Your Opportunity for Profit. At first glance, this business may seem hopelessly complicated for a person with no experience or skills in clock repair. Note carefully the first word—*old.* Old clocks are basically very simple devices. Many were homemade with hand tools years ago and cannot be called precision mechanisms by any means. If you enjoy tinkering, jump right into this one.

If you need encouragement, read what happened to Dave Harvey. He was a successful consultant working in a prestige job that earned him a five-figure salary. One day he bought an old clock at an auction and was hooked.

Dave got the clock working, which encouraged him to find others he could tinker with. In no time, he became something of a local expert others called when their old schoolroom or railroad clocks stopped working. Later on, he decided to stop the daily grind of going to the office, and opened a full-time clock repair service. He doesn't touch watches, or any timepiece younger than 50 years. Yet, his services are sought after by people from all over the country today.

What You Can Earn.   Figuring prices for your service can get a little tricky. Seldom will you be able to give a firm quote since each job will be unlike the others. Parts are not readily available at a set price, either. You'll have to get them by cannibalizing clocks that can't be repaired, or buying them from other collectors or dealers. Sometimes, you even make your own. But don't let this discourage you.

First, establish a base for your time as an expert—$10 an hour is a good figure once you've gotten some experience. You will be working on antiques and other valuable possessions, so price is seldom the deciding point. It is a curious fact that a low price can sometimes lose you business. People who value their property feel that a higher price is a measure of your experience and skill.

An example of what you can earn is as follows: 4 hours of work, say on a particular clock, comes to $40 at the $10 hourly rate. If you spent $26 acquiring parts, double that figure and add it to the $40. The total bill in this case comes to $92. Doubling the price of parts is quite acceptable as a markup figure. You have to do a lot more work getting them than merely ordering them from a stock catalog. Once established, Dave was able to make over $20,000 a year—at very pleasant work.

HOW TO BUILD YOUR WEALTH BASE

Here's What You Need.   What you really need most in this business is the liking and satisfaction that comes from making things work. You will need, of course, some small tools. Dave found these to be particularly helpful: needle-nose pliers, a set of small screwdrivers, a surgeon's hemostat, and a dental instrument known as a wiedelstat, which is a small chisel. As you work you will quickly discover what tools will speed your work. Then buy the best you can find.

How to Get Started. Get your hands on every book and other piece of information you can find relating to old clocks. Use your library to the fullest. Then, get some old clunkers that you can afford to botch, and try your hand at rebuilding and regulating them. A local chapter of the Antique Clock Association can be an excellent source of information, both technical and general.

How to Promote. When you have acquired some skill and confidence, start running some small ads in the local antique journals, and in the newsletters of nearby historical societies. Try your hand as a lecturer to local groups, particularly if you have a collection of clocks that can be displayed as part of your talk. Exposure of your talents in this fashion will help enormously in promoting your service.

Your Opportunity for Growth. This business, if aggressively pursued, can earn you a modest fortune in itself, particularly as you acquire a reputation. The management consultant we spoke of previously did just that. Or, if this seems unlikely in your circumstance, look upon the business as a relaxing way to work on your Wealth Base.

PARTY CONSULTANT

For Fun and Profit

Your Opportunity for Profit.   Louise Chester wanted to have the nicest possible party for her daughter's engagement. But she had no experience in planning such an affair. She had run her share of bridge and neighborhood parties, but an important and elaborate affair such as an engagement party had her in a panic.

Fortunately for Louise, a friend recommended Rose Carelli—a party consultant. Rose took charge of the event and saw to it that everything went smoothly, from ordering all the supplies to the final clean-up of the dishes. As a party consultant, Rose is the expert who has taken the time to find out what is proper and needed at parties and other formal gatherings.

You can be just this sort of expert, even if you've never attended big affairs. You can earn good money, meet some interesting people, and have fun doing it. How many people get paid for going to parties?

If you are outgoing and the sort of person who can take charge of things, and will spend some time looking up the proper procedures for each event, then this business is for you. You are the guiding hand—the party giver's manager. You may select the caterer, specify food and drinks, and even arrange for flowers and decorations—but you never handle a dirty dish or serve a drink.

What You Can Earn.   As other professionals do, you charge for your know-how and the actual time you spend planning and working. A base price for estimating your charges should be between $5 and $10 an hour. It is important to keep accurate records of your time. You'll probably be doing work for several clients at a single time and you will need to apportion your time accordingly. For instance—you might be booking a caterer for three different affairs, but a single phone call or visit will take care of all three. Using these time-saving methods, Rose usually counts on about $12,000 to $15,000 a year from this business.

HOW TO BUILD YOUR WEALTH BASE

Here's What You Need.   You don't need much more than a desire to do this kind of work, a liking for detail, and the ability to mix with all kinds of people. The party consultant's chief role is that of relieving the host and hostess of all the worrisome details of giving a party. About the only other thing you will need is some standard etiquette or party guide for reference.

How to Get Started.   Browse through as many books as you can find relating to parties, menu-planning and decorations. While reading through these sources, try to imagine yourself planning a party while applying the pointers you've picked up. Your worth comes not from what you can cram into your head, but in your knowledge of where to go for information you need. Spend some time with the telephone directory and get to know the various suppliers—caterers, florists, rental places, and the like.

After you feel confident, seek out a friend or relative who might be planning a large party. Offer to take charge—*without charge.* There is nothing like a real party to test you and to show off your talents to all the people attending the affair.

How to Promote.   Word-of-mouth advertising by those who have attended your early parties is the best way to build a list of clients. Remember, everyone who attends a party usually feels obligated to have a party of his own at some future date, and this fact keeps building your business from one success to another.

Try small ads in your newspaper. Key these ads to something special as: "Engagement and Wedding Parties" in June, "Halloween Parties" in the Fall, and so on.

Your Opportunity for Growth.   This business can grow, keeping its original form as a consultant only. Or, you may wish to expand dramatically, and enter the catering and rental business. Another lucrative area to enter is the business of arranging business meetings, conferences, and seminars. Here, you work with top company executives and make arrangements for hotel rooms and meeting space, plan meals and other social functions, and see to it that special services are provided as needed.

PATIO BUILDING

Simple Concrete Blocks Spell Profits for You

Your Opportunity for Profit.   Almost every homeowner decides, after a while, that his outdoor living would be improved with the addition of a patio in his backyard. This desire, plus a little know-how on your part, can be turned into a neat and profitable business.

Fortunately, you don't have to be an experienced mason contractor to build a very durable and attractive patio out of concrete blocks. These blocks are 8 by 16 inches in size, 2 inches thick, and come in a variety of colors. Although they can be cemented in place permanently, they are usually laid on a level bed of sand with no further cementing. Their weight keeps them in place, and winter frosts do not damage the finished patio.

What You Can Earn.   Generally, you will discuss with the customer what he has in mind, suggest some ideas of your own, and then work up an estimate of the cost of the job. However you charge, you must get back your materials cost, a fair payment for your time, plus an extra amount for your overhead, even though it starts out as a small business.

If the business appeals to you, but you have no idea of the time involved in a typical job, then build a concrete-block patio for yourself. The experience will be worth it and you will have a sample to show to prospective customers.

Don't be afraid to estimate your time at a minimum of $7 an hour for this work. Even though it is semi-skilled labor, you will find things cropping up to eat into your time estimate and you will need the extra cushion.

HOW TO BUILD YOUR WEALTH BASE

Here's What You Need.   The tools for patio building are simple and few—a level, a tape measure, some strong string, and some

digging tools. The simplest patio means nothing more than digging out a fairly level space, and then filling it with several inches
of level sand. On top of the sand lay the concrete blocks; the joints
are filled with more sand.

The finished paved area is level and sound. Strangely enough,
the sand joints act like a binder that makes the whole patio solid
like poured concrete, but with none of the disadvantages. There's
enough "give" in the sand joints to make the patio come through
winter after winter without any frost damage.

How to Get Started. If you have no idea how to start, or if you
want ideas for patterns of paving blocks, consult any number of
books on outdoor projects. Also, most handyman and garden
magazines carry features on these projects quite often.

How to Promote. Apart from word-of-mouth (after you've
completed a few jobs) the next best way to promote is to use small
announcements in your local newspaper. You won't sell anyone
on building a patio by just suggesting it. Rather, you will want to
have your name consistently exposed in the papers so that a prospect, once he decides to do the job, will think of you. Here are
some other tips:

- cruise new neighborhoods and recently completed develop-
  ments. A patio is usually high on a new homeowner's "want
  list."
- get to know the local building materials dealers. They are
  happy to recommend reliable local businessmen, particularly if it means that they can increase their sales of materials.

Your Opportunity for Growth. This is an ideal business for a
man who likes to work outdoors, and particularly if he has a
husky teenage son who feels the same. Spring will be the busiest
time of the year and you'll probably have to put off jobs for lack
of time. If you can, try to line up reliable workers willing to work
under your direction so that you can maximize your income during these busy months.

During the winter months, when it is impossible to work outdoors, you should consider some "indoor" businesses to keep your
Wealth Base growing. Any number of suitable ones can be found

in this book, and we urge you to read them all very carefully for ideas.

PHOTO DEVELOPING AND PRINTING

Profits from Pictures

Your Opportunity for Profit. Photography is one of the most popular hobbies in the country. Among the millions of picture *takers,* there are hundreds of thousands of picture *makers*—serious amateurs who have equipped a darkroom for developing and printing their own pictures. If you are among this group, then consider seriously the opportunity for profit in custom developing and printing.

You will not compete with the commercial labs with automated machinery. You will, by contrast, provide a custom service that no machine can ever offer. Neither will you compete with the professional photographer in town who is skilled in such custom work. He works only on his own pictures.

You will be the "lab" that the serious snapshooter turns to when he wants the very best—or something special that regular photofinishers do not handle. Every snapshooter has a special picture that he is especially proud of and would like to see it enlarged. Many times he is disappointed with the routine treatment given his negative by a mass-production lab. He will welcome the idea of giving his prize negative to a custom lab, such as the one you can run.

What You Can Earn. Get the scale of prices charged by your local camera store for various black and white services. You should consider doubling, or possibly tripling these prices. Where a big lab might charge $2 or $3 for an enlargement on mass production equipment, you should consider a minimum bill of $5.

You should offer a choice of printing papers, and you might even consider a dry-mount press for mounting photos. All of these extras can be charged for as custom work. A good evening's work in your darkroom should net you between $25 and $50, after you have paid for your supplies, light bill, and overhead.

People who have gone into the photo printing business have been able to make in excess of $25,000 a year, on a full-time basis.

HOW TO BUILD YOUR WEALTH BASE

Here's What You Need.   Obviously, you will need a darkroom able to handle regular black and white photographic work. This is the kind most amateurs have fixed up for themselves. Once you earn some money, you might want to consider adding some pieces of equipment that will make your work easier—a printing timer and meter, print dryer, dry-mount press, and densitometer to name only a few.

How to Get Started.   The first place to start is your local camera store, and the other stores that handle routine developing and printing through a commercial lab. If possible, try to get some prints made by the lab they use, and make some custom prints from the same negatives yourself. These samples are important in the presentation of your service.

How to Promote.   Make up a sample book with the regular and custom prints side by side. Work up a price schedule that gives enough margin so you can offer the dealer the same discount he enjoys from the commercial lab.

Take this presentation book and your story to these dealers and stores. Usually they've had experience with customers who were dissatisfied with mass-production work and would be willing to pay for something better. Your story and samples should sell them on your service. Your higher prices also means they earn more pushing your custom service, because they work on a percentage of the price.

If you offer to make custom prints they can display as samples, you'll find your service is easy to sell, not only to the dealer who has to take orders for you, but also to the ultimate customer who wants something better than routine lab work.

Your Opportunity for Growth.   You can't grow fantastically in any custom type business. To handle the increased business, you'd have to install automatic equipment. This destroys the very thing you are selling—careful craftsmanship with individual attention to each print.

You can charge enough for your work, and do enough of it yourself to provide a respectable spare-time income. If you have a friend who also does careful work—perhaps a fellow member of the local camera club—you can farm your overflow work out to him and make more money. You might also consider the custom framing business described elsewhere in this book as a natural addition for building your Wealth Base.

PICTURE FRAMING SERVICE

Put Yourself in This Profit Picture

Your Opportunity for Profit.   If someone values a picture, diploma, certificate, or some other document, they are often willing to pay quite a bit to have it framed in a suitable manner.

It is possible to buy an inexpensive frame in a variety store, but such a frame will seldom do justice to the item being framed. Many times, the picture, or item being framed, becomes a very important part of the overall decorative scheme of a room where it will hang, and so must be made in just the right size and color.

In this business, you frame a variety of items according to the specific wishes of your customer, or more likely, to your own ideas of how to show off the item to best advantage.

The growing interest in old photographs and prints (see the

"Nostalgia" Business) provides a ready market for the person in the custom framing business.

What You Can Earn. Your prices will depend on your cost of materials and on your time. There is more to framing than slipping a frame behind a piece of glass. For this reason, it is not unusual for a framing job to run $15 or $20 for an art print, a certificate or diploma, or some award that will be displayed in a company executive's office.

No hard and fast rules can be given because a lot will depend on the type of work you do, the materials involved, and what kind of clients you will be dealing with. A company that has just received some award will spend a lot more than an individual.

HOW TO BUILD YOUR WEALTH BASE

Here's What You Need. The most important need is framing material. The frame stock is available at lumber yards and in art stores; the mat boards, backing cardboard, and other items usually found only in the latter. Don't overlook the wholesale supplier when you begin to buy in sufficient quantities.

If a source of supply is not near, a good place to shop by mail is Arthur Brown, 57 West 44th Street, New York, N.Y. 10022. Write for their catalog. At an art store like this you will also find booklets on the art of framing. Your local librarian can also help you out.

How to Get Started. Check out the most likely sources of business leads for your framing business. These places will include art stores, print and book shops, and photographers' studios. You will also have to invest both the time and money in making samples to show to prospective customers. You will find that most people will select a few basic styles, but it is always important to give them a wide selection of styles to choose from. People do not like to feel that they must select from a limited number of choices.

How to Promote. Small consistent advertising is the key here. Consider both newspaper classified and telephone directory advertising.

Make contact with a local photographer—particularly one that does a lot of work on school yearbooks. Invariably, the photos they take are ordered by parents, and without too much selling you can get them to order the photo framed . . . by you. Your promotion can be nothing more complicated or expensive than a simple printed announcement which the photographer includes with his proofs, and also earns him a small commission. You will have to work out a rate, but a fair rule of thumb is to give him 10 to 15% of the selling price.

Your Opportunity for Growth. From a part-time business growing out of your basement, you can expand to a full-time framing shop. This business is an excellent addition to the photo printing business discussed elsewhere in this book.

PLANT CONTAINER MAKING

Your Profits Will Bloom

Your Opportunity for Profit. Next time you walk into a "posh" restaurant, a well-appointed office, or an elegant home, look around at the plants that are used as important parts of the overall decorating scheme. Seldom will you find these plants growing in ordinary flower pots or containers that are so familiar in garden shops and nurseries.

Instead, you will see custom-made containers. Each is built according to the specifications of the person responsible for the decorating plan. Someone has to make these containers. If you like working with a variety of materials—if you enjoy working out problems of design and construction—then you can find making custom plant containers a fascinating spare-time activity that can bring surprising financial rewards.

What You Can Earn. Because containers vary so, it is impossible to give anything but guidelines as to what you should charge.

After reviewing the plan, estimate the cost of the materials involved. Your own experience will guide you in estimating the number of work-hours involved. A simple redwood box container, knocked together in a few minutes, is worth $3. An elaborate trough for a restaurant is easily worth $100. These hours should be charged for at a rate you have set for your skill with tools.

All things considered, you should get back all the material costs plus $5 to $10 an hour for your time spent. Don't forget to include the design time as well as the time spent in the workshop.

HOW TO BUILD YOUR WEALTH BASE

Here's What You Need.   We'll assume you're a hobbiest who likes to work with tools. If so, you probably have all the tools and "shop" you need to start this business.

How to Get Started.   Begin by collecting all the reference material you can on plant containers, flower boxes, and the like. Most garden books and magazines will have chapters or sections on containers for all types of plants.

And, don't be afraid to copy! If you see something that strikes your imagination, make a quick on-the-spot sketch of the container. The value of this file increases with each addition. Most professional designers, whether they are architects, interior decorators, or artists, all have an idea file like this to which they refer for inspiration.

How to Promote.   Promoting your business can take many forms, depending on the kind of operation you decide to run. You may decide to run off several dozen simple planter boxes and tubs, and display them for sale in a "retail" type of operation. If you live in an open area, and zoning ordinances permit, this "retail location" can be your own yard. In such case, your major promotion will probably be an attractive sign, visible from the main road.

In addition, you may invest in small space advertising in your local paper—particularly in the spring when people think of gardening. If you want to concentrate on custom work to order, then there are people you should cultivate. High on the list is the local garden shop or nursery. Work an arrangement with the owner so that you will be recommended or your work displayed, in return for a commission.

Make up a fact sheet describing the range of your services and mail it to local architects, building contractors, and landscape designers.

Finally, you should contact your local garden club. Many times they are responsible for beautifying areas as part of a civic project, and their plantings are often done in containers of one sort or another.

For the established builder: consider selling your wares in knocked-down "kit" form through the mail. Mail order can be very profitable. *The Franklin Letter,* a monthly newsletter for ambitious individuals, makes available to subscribers a variety of helps for making money in mail order. A year's subscription is only $18, and worth it many times in hints and advice. Send your check to *The Franklin Letter*, Box 95, Demarest, New Jersey 07627.

Your Opportunity for Growth.   As your reputation grows, you may find yourself with more business than you can handle, particularly during certain times of the year. If the workload is constantly beyond your two hands, then you'll have to seek additional hands. With luck, and plenty of hard work, you might even grow to the point where you do all the selling and planning, while all the construction work is done by your employees.

Combine this business with other "building-type" businesses—antique restoration, chair caning, and the like. Flower arranging is another one to consider.

POOL CLEANING AND TESTING

Dip into These Profits

Your Opportunity for Profit.   The swimming pool, whether it is above or below ground requires a lot of maintenance. In fact, most towns require that it be tested regularly for chlorine content. Most people who install a swimming pool plan to relax in it, and are not especially interested in doing the work required to keep it up.

In spring, the pool must be cleaned of debris, often painted, and the surrounding cement must be patched where frost has taken its toll. During the summer, regular maintenance requires care of the pump, filters, water supply connections, drains, and even the surrounding grounds. In the fall, some pools are drained, others are covered and supplied with either logs or inflated inner tubes to take up the expansion when ice forms.

All of this means business for you, a sun tan, and occasional dips, to boot.

What You Can Earn. Sell a service contract—and you will insure a steady source of business most of the season. Such a contract would include most of what was described above, and could even include such extras as swimming and scuba lessons if you have the ability. Obviously, each contract would have different specifications, but if you were to take on the three-season service we outlined, you could charge $150. Of course, your income will depend on the number of pools in your area, the number of contracts you sell, and how many you can handle in a season.

Consider this for a general guide-line: it should be easy to make at least 3 stops a day, and you should visit each client at least once a week during the swimming season. This means you can handle, comfortably, 15 clients for such routine maintenance, at a gross income of $4500. Of course, you can earn more with the many special situations that occur that are not covered by your contract.

HOW TO BUILD YOUR WEALTH BASE

Here's What You Need. Each job will require different equipment, but all of it is basic and inexpensive. Paint brushes, a cement trowel, a large scrub brush, chlorine tester, and basic garden tools if you are also caring for the surrounding grounds. Of course, you'll need a pair of trunks and some sun-tan lotion.

How to Get Started. Cruise your neighborhood and make a list of every address with a pool. You could also visit the town building inspector and ask him for the names of people with permits for pools. This is public information, and you are entitled to it.

Then, early in March, start ringing door bells. Tell these pool owners that you have a service specifically for them, and emphasize that it will allow them to relax and enjoy the pool, rather than become its janitor.

How to Promote.   Because you can spot your customers quickly, the best way to promote is to either make a call on them directly, or send out simple post cards announcing the service. Classified ads are of little value here.

Your Opportunity for Growth.   Obviously, this is a seasonal business, but you can expand by adding help and looking for more customers. Don't overlook the swim clubs that have sprung up all over the country. These can result in large contracts for the right service. You might add the patio building service to your service and even consider lawn maintenance and general home cleaning.

PREPARATION WORK FOR HOME PAINTERS

Making the Job Easy for Others

Your Opportunity for Profit.   You can see 'em every weekend when the weather is good—the determined homeowners hanging from ladders with paint brushes in their hands.

"Anyone can paint a house," they say, "all you need to do is slap on the paint."

A professional painter would be aghast. From long experience he knows that the most important part of any painting job is the preparation work—the cleaning, scraping, patching, and repairing that should be done before you even dip a brush in a can of paint. Most amateurs are so anxious to see a new coat of paint on their house that they neglect this all important step.

Knowing that most homeowners are unable or unwilling to take the time to do this job, suggests a business you can set up that will do this chore for the amateur painter. He can still save substantially on his paint job by doing it himself, and he has the added assurance that a good prep job will add extra years of good looks to his efforts with a brush.

What You Can Earn.   Figuring the cost of your service is fairly simple, but you must have some idea of what local painters get for a complete paint job. Let's assume that an average quote for painting a typical house is $700 in your area. If you figure that about $100 of this goes for paint, then the painter is charging $600 for his labor. About a quarter of the time should be charged off to prep work which means that this part of the job is worth about $150. If a homeowner adds this cost to the price of the paint, he is still ahead of the game, particularly when you realize that he will have to paint less frequently.

HOW TO BUILD YOUR WEALTH BASE

Here's What You Need.   You'll need most of the things a good painter carries to the job, with the exception of paint and paint-brushes. Get yourself a good extension ladder, an assortment of scrapers, putty knives, a calking gun, and dusting brushes. Check into getting some liability insurance in case you accidentally put out a window with your ladder.

How to Get Started.   Get to know the local paint store dealer, the owner of the hardware store with a big paint department, and even a local painter or two. Usually the store will permit you to tack up a note on a bulletin board announcing the service. They might even talk up your business if you can convince them that it will mean increased paint sales for them. And don't forget to spread the word among your friends. You don't need many jobs to stay busy all season.

Another hint is to drive around in early Spring looking for

homes in need of paint. A knock on the door, or a card in the mailbox might easily get you a couple of jobs.

Professional painters can often use your help when they get extremely busy. It's a delicate area, though, because many painters will think of you as a direct competition. You might be able to work something out with a friend, however.

How to Promote.   Start running small display ads early in the Spring in your local newspaper or Shopper publication. Stress your essential message: you do the dull part of the job . . . they have the fun part. Also remind them constantly that a good prep job pays for itself in a longer lasting paint job.

Your Opportunity for Growth.   The natural expansion of this business is into general painting. But, before you decide to take such a step, consider what you will be doing. For example:

- you will immediately lose the homeowner-painter that was your previous customer
- you will immediately face the competition of all the other established painters in your locality

If these pointers don't deter you, good luck. You might, however, think long on keeping the business as it is—a prep business strictly, and never touch a paintbrush. Advertise more aggressively, recruit some college kids during the summer months, and clean up as the homeowners' clean-up man before painting.

You may, of course, add other services to your list. Building a patio and even acting as the handyman consultant can be an ideal way to expand your Wealth Base building capacity.

PRINTING SERVICES

Simple Equipment Brings Big Profits

Your Opportunity for Profit.   Michael Solomon was the production manager for a small advertising agency, with the responsibility for buying all the printing for his company's clients. Mike had started out a few years earlier as a printer and, although he moved up into management, he never lost his interest in printing, and the money that could be made.

Seeing that a lot of the printing he was buying could be handled on a small press—one that would easily fit in his basement—he took the plunge. With less than $100 down, and payment of about $30 a month, he bought a used multilith press. Mike soon became a valuable supplier to his agency, as well as an important employee. Of course, he soon got business from other sources, and had to hire someone to run the press for him part-time. He now has all of the equipment he needs for a complete printing service —platemaker, cutter, collater, and folder—all bought and paid for out of profits from his part-time venture.

What You Can Earn. The key to success in this business is specialization. Mike specialized in "utility" printing. While other printers competed with each other for the expensive, quality work, Mike sought out the simple, short-run black-and-white work that most printers feel is unprofitable. Mike has few problems with fussy buyers, and most of his jobs are cash-and-carry—something that is hard to do when you run big multi-color jobs.

Prices for work will vary all over the country, so it is impossible to cite cash amounts that will be meaningful to all. The best way to establish a price is with the aid of the Printing Trades Blue Book, published by A. F. Lewis & Co., 853 Broadway, New York City. This helpful guide is published in thirty three regional editions and gives up-to-date data on regional prices as well as names and addresses of dealers, paper houses, trade associations and all the other sources a printer would need.

In his second year, Mike made over $7000 profit, and seldom put his hands on his basement press.

HOW TO BUILD YOUR WEALTH BASE

Here's What You Need. This is a business where you need some know-how. Many vocational schools give excellent printing courses for adults during the evening.

You will need a press, and sources for paper, plates and binding. The yellow pages and the Blue Book will give you the leads for these sources. A good used press can be bought on favorable terms from most printing equipment brokers. Often, press manufacturers take trade-ins and can offer used buys.

How to Get Started.   Once you have the equipment, and know how to run it adequately, you have the first source of promotion right at your fingertips—your press. Have a local artist, or advertising agency, design a flyer for you and mail it out to everyone who would have a need for your kind of printing. This includes all manufacturers, large stores, hospitals, and even schools. Of course, ad agencies need your help, too. You might even be able to trade a few free jobs with an agency in return for their help in designing and writing a mailing piece for you.

How to Promote.   Classified ads in the local newspaper, and sales calls on your prospects are about the best way of digging up business. If the local Jaycees or Rotary has a bulletin, do the printing, at "cost" to get the word out to the merchants. Of course, continue to send out mailers, and make sure that any friends you have in business know about the service.

Your Opportunity for Growth.   Obviously, you can add presses and people, but there are other ways of increasing your income with this as a Wealth Base. The messenger service, described in this book, is an ideal addition. Be sure to set it up so that your driver makes regular stops at good customers, whether they have work, or not. This way, they will come to expect you, and will make sure that you get every job. You might also consider the advertising distribution service—where you now print what you are distributing. The blueprint business and mailing services are also natural additions to this business.

PRIVATE TRANSPORTATION SERVICE

You're on the Road to Success

Your Opportunity for Profit. There's a big difference between running a private transportation service and a taxi business. Taxi businesses depend on day-to-day calls for their money, and have to be ready to take anyone anywhere.

Not so with this private transportation service. Instead of going after the "one-time" customer, you set about getting contracts or long-term agreements to chauffer people at regular intervals. Therefore, you look for the person who has, let us say, a regular weekly appointment with a doctor; the working person who doesn't drive; the business that requires regular pick-ups or deliveries that can be handled by a driver in a private car; and so on. The advantage of going after this kind of business is obvious . . .

- You know beforehand who you are going to transport and where he is going.
- You can sometimes arrange your schedule to double up on your trips for extra income.
- You can plan your time for leisure, or other money-making activities.

Children with handicaps often need to be transported to special schools, and the cost of this transportation is borne by the school system. Private bus companies usually handle this business, which is let out by competitive bidding. If a single child is involved, a regular bus company will not bid for the business, because it would seldom be profitable. In a situation like this, the child's own parent can bid on the business and actually get paid for driving his own child to school.

What You Can Earn. Your rate has to pay you for your time, for the use of your car, gasoline, insurance, and the like. The government tax depreciation laws allow 10¢ a mile as the cost of running a car. Using this as a rough figure, you can compute your costs for the distance between two points. Obviously, a long run on the open highway should cost you less than a lot of stop-and-start driving in the city. Figure time to be worth at least $4 per hour, plus a pro-rated amount for the other expenses.

Your earnings can vary a great deal depending on the type of contract you negotiate. For transporting a handicapped child to school, it is not unusual to get $50 a week—and this is often for a relatively short trip twice a day.

HOW TO BUILD YOUR WEALTH BASE

Here's What You Need.   Your basic piece of equipment is your car—preferably a late model station wagon. Before starting, double-check your insurance policy with your agent. You'll probably have to pay a few dollars extra to get full liability coverage when you carry people for hire. Generally speaking, no other licenses are required, but be sure to check this with your local motor vehicle bureau, or police department.

How to Get Started.   Do some basic research in your town to discover the number of people who could use reliable transportation services if they were available. Think of all the handicapped people needing to be transported to schools and doctors' offices, and even to work. Usually, your telephone directory will give you a good idea of the number of doctors' offices and special schools in the area. Don't be afraid to call the receptionist in the various offices and ask how the doctors' patients are transported for treatment.

How to Promote.   Classified ads and a listing in the yellow pages are a must for promoting this business. A small ad can be just as effective as a large one. You're not "selling," rather you are listing your name and phone number for reference.

In addition, try these sure-fire leads:

- send a dignified announcement or personal letter to the various doctors in your area. Many of them have regular patients who need reliable transportation.
- call on the principals of your local schools. They can tell you what sort of transportation agreements they have for taking children to special schools. Find out when the next

bids will be advertised, and how much the previous successful bidders have charged. This is public information, and you have the right to request and receive the details.

Your Opportunity for Growth.   As you gain more and more customers, you obviously will not be able to handle all the requests. Add helpers to your staff, making sure that your charges are enough not only to pay the people who work for you (and who are using their own cars), but also to give you that something extra called profit for your work in building the business.

PROSPECT LIST COMPILATION

Getting Customers for Others Makes Money for You

Your Opportunity for Profit.   Every business must have access to new customers, and most businesses actually will make up lists for promotional work. Even if they do not sell their products thru the mail, many businessmen find it helpful to keep in touch with buyers by making regular mailings.

You can make quite a bit of money by putting these lists together. And the number of businesses for which you can work is almost endless. You can work for the actual users of such lists, and you can contract with local mailing houses to do list compilation for their customers.

When Doris Williamson decided to supplement her husband's income, she began working as a typist for a large list compiling house. Quickly realizing that she could offer a similar compilation service to smaller businesses, she soon opened an office in her basement recreation room. Her first assignment came from an advertising agency which wanted a list of manufacturing plants within a 30 mile radius of its office. Doris made use of the directories in her public library, and simply typed the required information on 3 × 5 cards for the agency. The librarian had shown her exactly which directories to use for this money-making assignment.

What You Can Earn.   The prices you can charge will vary with the amount of research necessary to come up with the names. In Doris' first assignment, it was simply a matter of locating the companies in a directory, and transcribing them onto labels. For this task, she charged 2½¢ a name. She has a minimum compilation charge of $25 per thousand.

Now, this may not seem like a lot of money, but when Doris made this first list, she also made a duplicate, which is available to anyone else for the same price of $25 per thousand. So far, she has rented it to nine other companies. Each time she types it, she is asked to "slug" it with a different person's title. For example, one user wanted to reach the purchasing agents of these companies, so Doris typed, "Attention: Purchasing Agent" on every envelope she addressed.

This list "pyramiding" has helped Doris to net over $8,000 a year for part-time work.

HOW TO BUILD YOUR WEALTH BASE

Here's What You Need.   All you really need is a typewriter in good working order, and a place to work. This can be a corner of a room, but you should have a place in which to store the lists you are making for future rental.

How to Get Started.   Contact every store in town. Tell them of your service, and explain that you can prepare, and maintain a mailing list for them at a modest cost. Be sure to point out the value of such a list in the promotion of sales and other special merchandising events.

You should also contact the following businesses:

- mailing houses
- advertising agencies
- market research services

- manufacturers
- manufacturers representatives and wholesalers of all types

How to Promote. Because you will be part of the direct mail profession, you should use this medium extensively to promote your service.

The first thing to do, of course, is to make up complete lists of prospects for yourself. Then, prepare a simple notice of your service, and mail it out. Be sure to include a post-paid reply card for the respondent to use when he is interested in having you "cut" a mailing list for him.

Your Opportunity for Growth. Initially, your business will all be handled by typewriter. That is, the lists will be typed, and re-typed manually. As soon as you can afford it, be sure to investigate an inexpensive addressing machine. One of the best for this type of operation is made by Elliot. Their equipment is modular in design, and you can buy a basic machine, to which you can add equipment as you grow without obsoleting your original purchase.

At this point, you will be in a position to offer almost a full range of list services, but you may also consider these businesses which we have covered elsewhere in the book:

- advertising distribution services, Simple lettershop services, Mimeograph services, Freelance researcher.

PUBLIC BOOKKEEPER

Small Checks Add Up Fast to a Big Income

Your Opportunity for Profit. Each year about a half million new businesses are started. The majority have several things in common—they are usually small, and their record keeping is a mess. As a public bookkeeper, you can perform vital bookkeeping services for scores of small businessmen from your home, by mail, and earn substantial fees, prestige, and other benefits that accrue to a professional.

Your opportunity here lies with the small businessman—the man who cannot afford the services of a full-time bookkeeper, and who usually is too pressed to do an adequate job himself. He will gladly pay an outsider to take over this job when you show him that good records can save him your monthly fee several times over.

What You Can Earn.   An income of $10,000 a year is easily possible, even if you live in a small town. The average client pays $3 to $5 a month. A few larger clients will pay up to $30 a month (which is still only a tiny fraction of what they would have to pay a full-time person). With proper mix of clients, you can easily earn $900 to $1000 a month on 75 clients or so. These 75 clients can be handled with no more than a few hours work each day.

HOW TO BUILD YOUR WEALTH BASE

Here's What You Need.   You will need some basic know-how of simple bookkeeping, the kind that is necessary for ordinary retail shops or service businesses. A supply of forms and envelopes will complete your inventory of business supplies. If you have no bookkeeping experience at all, you might want to investigate the materials available from Auditax Systems, P. O. Box 34741, Los Angeles, California 90034.

How to Get Started.   The secret here is to systematize your own work schedules to permit you to handle many clients with the minimum of fuss and bother. That means an efficient filing system (a folder for each client), a big calendar pad that can take loads of follow-up notes, and pre-printed forms and envelopes to eliminate as much routine typing as possible.

Each month, your clients will fill out and return your pre-printed forms which have spaces for money taken in and money paid out. You take this information and tabulate it according to standard bookkeeping practice, and then send your client a copy of your summary each week or month. At the end of the year you complete his books with an annual profit and loss statement, and even complete his tax return if requested. Information on the tax preparation business is included elsewhere in this book.

How to Promote.   Your first clients will be local businessmen, particularly the smaller retailers and service shops. Call on them directly. Later, you expand your business with a mail campaign. New businesses generally have to register their names at the local courthouse in most states. These names are available from various mailing list houses, and you can request them by locality for a slight extra charge. This way you can reach hundreds of nearby businessmen, who probably haven't even faced the problem of bookkeeping as yet, and offer them an incredibly low-cost bookkeeping service by mail.

Your Opportunity for Growth.   With the enormous numbers of new businesses being formed each day, there is really no limit to what you can earn. If you generate your business by mail, all you have to do is to solicit clients further and further away. You won't get out of your own state before you'll have to think of adding help to your business to handle the volume of work.

RECORDING SPECIAL EVENTS

The Sound of Money

Your Opportunity for Profit.   Everybody has pictures taken at weddings. Flashbulbs pop at picnics, parties, and other family events. But, pictures are only partly effective in preserving memories.

When the bride says, "I do," no picture can ever capture that moment and make it live like the moment the words were spoken. Here's where you come in . . . and make a welcome profit.

With simple, relatively inexpensive portable recording equipment, you can record these once-in-a-lifetime events and preserve the sound forever. While many people have such recorders, at such events no one involved in the activity will have the time or the inclination to make a recording. A lot of people own cameras, but they usually hire a professional photographer to take pictures at times like these. These "living memories" can be every bit as profitable as pictures are to the photographer.

What You Can Earn.   Your problems in establishing a price are also identical to that of the photographer. You have to invest a fair amount of time and some materials in order to make the first set (or first tape). Duplicates are relatively inexpensive since they involve little time and materials. If your clients want only one copy of a tape, then your price might seem a bit steep. If you sell them on the idea of several duplicates at the same time, then the price per tape is considered lessened. You can earn up to $50 for your work if you get a good recording, and you get orders for several duplicates from the relatives of the bride and groom.

HOW TO BUILD YOUR WEALTH BASE

Here's What You Need.   All you need is a battery-powered cassette tape recorder. While even a fairly inexpensive model will give adequate service, you should consider buying a fairly good instrument at the start. Look at the tape recorders sold to businessmen for recording meetings and conferences. These models usually have an automatic volume control that makes recording various sound levels both automatic and foolproof. Such a recorder can cost less than $100.

How to Get Started.   As a start, take your recorder to a wedding, a christening, or even a local political meeting. Practice getting the recording done without wasting tape on meaningless background noise. Remember—the listener can only *hear* what is going on, and any sound must be instantly recognizable by the listener. If you want, you can add your own very limited comments, such as, "the bride is now stepping out of the car". Be sparing in comments such as these since your clients are not buying *your* voice or comments.

When you feel confident in handling your recorder, take it to the wedding of a friend or someone known to you. After the couple has returned from their honeymoon, give them the tape at no charge. They'll be dazzled, and will probably tell everyone they know about your service. This word-of-mouth advertising is your best start.

How to Promote.   Keep your eye on the newspaper for engagement announcements and special events. Call these prospects and tell them of your service. Give as a reference the couple that got your first free tape.

Local theatrical groups are often good prospects for tapes. People who take part in amateur plays enjoy the spotlight. Many of them would pay gladly for this permanent remembrance of their favorite performance.

Also keep in touch with local service clubs. Many of them have speakers at regular intervals, who would appreciate having a recording of the speech they give on some occasion.

Advertising can be best handled on the classified advertising pages of your newspaper, or small space advertising on the society pages where the wedding and engagement announcements usually appear. Check where the florists and photographers advertise and follow their lead.

Your Opportunity for Growth.   Your biggest problem in growing will be handling conflicting assignments. Most weddings take place on weekends, and you can only be at one place at a time. Therefore, you should find some competent assistant to help you out of spots like this. Your spouse is ideal since you don't have to worry about a competitor in the business.

For selling duplicates, you can send your tapes to an outside lab. Usually, they have better equipment than you might want to acquire, and make better copies.

You might even consider joining with a photographer. If he is already well established, much of the selling will be done for you. You will have to work out a commission arrangement with him for such help, but your selling costs drop to zero in this case.

REMEMBRANCE SERVICE

Make Money by Being a Thoughtful Person

Your Opportunity for Profit.   Ask the next five men you meet the exact date of their wedding anniversary. Also ask them what happened when they forgot to remember the last one.

What does this suggest? Simply that most of us are forgetful, and that an opportunity exists for becoming the other fellow's "memory." Instead of trusting to your memory, however, you will have it all down on paper. You simply notify clients in advance when they want to be reminded of some special event. It's as easy as that.

Take the case of Myron Kraus, now retired in California, who had a dozen grandchildren to remember. Now, when their birthdays are imminent, he gets a card reminding him of the fact about 10 days before the date. This gives him plenty of time to get a card or gift and send it off to the particular grandchild.

What You Can Earn.   A dollar a remembrance is a good charge. Of course, if you work out something with a business firm that remembers anniversaries (such as an insurance office) then you can cut your price for this service. Why don't they mark their calendars in advance and do the remembering themselves? A few, orderly minded people will do so, and will never become your customers. But human nature being what it is, we all like the easy way to do things. A postcard coming in the mail is a genuine reminder. Even if you marked it on the calendar, you could *forget to look at the calendar!*

HOW TO BUILD YOUR WEALTH BASE

Here's What You Need.   Your equipment will consist of a supply of postcards, and a three-ring binder with 12 tabs that can be used to separate the months. This is a trifling investment that can earn a surprisingly high return for your time.

How to Get Started.   It's hard to pick a particular market to go after when starting this business. Everyone has a need for it. Perhaps the simplest is to ask the owner of a stationery store if you can put up a small card near his card section. This should attract people who have people to remember, and should also stimulate the sale of greetings once your business is rolling.

Be sure to talk about your service to as many people as possible to start the word-of-mouth advertising going. Tell your neighbors, coworkers, lodge members, and even relatives.

Set up your remembrance book with one tab for each month with plenty of paper behind each tab. As you get a customer, enter the date he wants to be reminded under the appropriate month. The date you put in is the date on which *you* will send your reminder card. Each customer will probably want a different time lag. Your postcard reminder simply says, "Fred's birthday is September 25th," or something equally short.

How to Promote.   In addition to the contact with the stationery store, a good approach is to run occasional classified ads in the "personals" column. Your big clients will be among businesses that make a point of remembering anniversaries. You can arrange with such companies to take on the actual work of sending out the remembrances.

Your Opportunity for Growth.   In the beginning, you will merely send out reminders to your customers that an anniversary is in the offing. They will handle the rest of the details. Later, you can expand the service by actually sending cards, flowers, candy, or whatever else may be asked for, and thereby take over the whole job of remembering an anniversary date.

An adjunct to the business would be to offer a gift shopping service. This is particularly welcome to some men who feel ill at ease when buying articles of clothing for their wives.

Because you will be working with a typewriter, you can also offer a typing service. If you have added any duplicating equipment, such as a mimeograph, be sure to put it to work on a "jobbing" basis for people with such a need.

REPAIR SHOP PICK-UP AND DELIVERY SERVICE

Pick Up Profits for Yourself, Too

Your Opportunity for Profit. As an experiment, take a quick look at the yellow pages of your telephone directory. Quickly list the different repair shops located in your town—and count the number of businesses that repair TV's, lawnmowers, electrical appliances, sporting goods, machinery and small tools, office equipment, and so on.

Chances are, in no time, you will have a rather large list. The longer the list, the greater your opportunity for profit. Here's the secret: few of these businesses can afford a full-time pick-up and delivery service of its own. With a small truck, or even a station wagon, you can become the pick-up and delivery service for a number of businesses. With enough of businesses in your area, you can even keep a small fleet of trucks busy.

What You Can Earn. The secret of making money in this business is to get as many businesses as possible to use your service to keep both truck and driver busy throughout the day. Your charges to your clients will have to recover your truck expenses and driver's time, even if you're the driver in the beginning. And, of course, you have to have a profit on top of that. You'll have to work out a scale of charges for the various items you pick up, most of which will probably be charged back to the ultimate customer who is having an item repaired. A typical pick-up and delivery of a TV set should cost him about $3 on his bill, most of which goes to you, the repair shop keeping a small part of it for their expense in arranging for the pick up and delivery.

This can become a profitable business earning you a good five-figure income once it becomes established. Unlike the usual trucking business, which is very competitive, there is virtually no competition in this area because regular truckers simply don't like this type of business. They prefer working with larger clients who have a lot of similar packages to be delivered at a time.

HOW TO BUILD YOUR WEALTH BASE

Here's What You Need.   The obvious need is some sort of delivery vehicle. Your own station wagon, or a rented pick-up panel truck can serve nicely in this business. Check with your insurance man about any additional liability coverage you may need. After all, you want to be protected if you happen to drop a customer's TV while it's being unloaded.

How to Get Started.   Starting this business has already been described—do some research in the classified pages of your telephone directory and your newspaper for likely repair shops and services that can use your service.

How to Promote.   There is only one way to promote this business—personal calls on the prospects your research has revealed. Here is the selling point to use on them: a reliable pick-up and delivery service enables them to give better service to their customers, and also saves time dealing with people delivering items to the shop. Remind them that their most valuable time is the time they spend fixing things that are brought in for repair, and not the time out front with a customer.

Most people prefer to have things picked up and delivered; so they can increase their business by using your service. And, finally, it is entirely fair to charge a nominal delivery charge back to the customer so that the repairman doesn't really spend any money at all on your service. It pays for itself and increases his business, too!

Your Opportunity for Growth.   Once you have some experience in this business, you'll find many ways to increase your growth rate. The obvious way is to add more trucks and drivers. True, you'll be increasing your expenses for payroll and so on, but your over-riding profit from a number of trucks will keep you on the high road to profit. Be sure to read the section on messenger service. They are alike in many ways, and can be combined, if desired.

RESTAURANT CALL-IN SERVICE

Food for Thought . . . and Profit

Your Opportunity for Profit.   Today, interest in different kinds of food is very strong. Consider how many Chinese, Italian and other foreign type restaurants abound in certain neighborhoods. And, consider that each usually has several specials each day, and unless the customer comes in and reads the menu, he will never know when his favorite dish is being served.

Here's where the Diners' Call-In Service makes money for you . . . and the restaurant. You sell your services to each one of the major types of restaurants in your neighborhood, and simply answer questions over the phone about the menu as the calls come in. And, you also book reservations for the restaurants. You can also take orders for food "to-go."

What You Can Earn.   You will have to cover out-of-pocket expenses, of course, and charge also for your time on the phone. Rather than make it a fixed hourly rate for each restaurant, you should establish a base rate per week for the service. You might even consider offering a lower rate and taking a commission on all reservations and "to-go" orders, but the bookkeeping can often cost more than the bother is worth. We suggest that you stick to a flat "service" charge, and $50 a month for the complete service, per restaurant is certainly a bargain for the restaurant owner.

HOW TO BUILD YOUR WEALTH BASE

Here's What You Need.   All you need is a telephone. Be sure to get one with line expansion facilities so that when business grows, you can add an extra person to another phone. Obviously, this is an ideal business to operate at home, but DON'T use your personal phone—be sure to have a separate line.

How to Get Started.   Go thru the yellow pages, and pick out one each of the major types of restaurants—French, Italian, Chinese, Japanese, Steak House, etc. Then, visit each one personally and tell your story. Because your market will be rather small, we suggest that you make personal calls rather than writing or phoning. It's much easier to sell a service on a face-to-face basis than thru the mail or over the phone.

When you get enough restaurants to make it worth while, contact the phone company and have them put in the lines.

How to Promote.   Once you have signed up your restaurant-customers, you will be promoting to the diner himself. Have a card printed, telling your story, and listing the restaurants you represent, and distribute it everywhere. This includes the restaurants themselves, plus stuffers in supermarket shopping bags, and even having them distributed door-to-door by after-school workers. Be sure to contact the editor of your local newspaper, and have him do a story on your enterprise. After all, your restaurant customers are his advertisers, and he should be anxious to lend a free hand. A big ad in the phone book classified can net a lot of calls here.

Your Opportunity for Growth.   As we mentioned, you can add another phone answerer or two, but you should really consider becoming a booking agent for large dinners and banquets at your client restaurants. Contact all the local fraternal groups and offer the service, and in return collect a fee from the restaurant for placing the business. Ten percent of the total bill is often a fair fee, and easily negotiated with the owner.

RESUME SERVICE

Jobs for Others Means Money for You

Your Opportunity for Profit.   Americans, unlike many other people in the world, are constantly changing jobs. Many times it's the spirit of achievement, advancement, and a quest for the better things in life. Sometimes, during periods of distress, layoffs, and cutbacks, it's a matter of necessity. Yet, most people who are looking to change their jobs don't really know how to go about it in a professional way.

The first step in preparing for a better job is to make up a *resume*—a carefully thought-out description of one's education, and experience. A well-done resume attracts the attention of a prospective employer, and makes him want to know more about the job-seeker.

As often happens, a chance event puts a person in business, such as the case of Harry Lustig. He worked as a low-pay clerk in a printing plant and was asked by a friend to have his resume printed—"as a favor." When Harry read over this friend's resume, his fresh eye uncovered many weaknesses his job-hunting friend had not considered. After all, who can really be objective about writing his own resume?

Harry suggested some constructive changes. His friend appreciated the advice, and was even more delighted when he landed a much better job. Soon Harry was getting requests from others, both friends and strangers who heard about him. In time, Harry left the dull routine of his clerical job, and set himself up as a job consultant, handling all the details of writing and printing resumes for job-seekers.

What You Can Earn.   You make money two ways in this business: one for the actual writing of the resume, and the other for the duplication of the finished product. Your charges for the actual writing should be based on an hourly rate—the time it takes to interview your client and get required information, and the actual time it takes you to work up the resume. A fair price for this work is $7 to $10 an hour. An average resume will take about an hour per page to prepare.

When you arrange to duplicate the resumes, look for an "offset" printer who specializes in short runs of printing. Take the printer's charges and mark them up by 25%. If you have to pay a professional typist to prepare the original copy going to the printer, add these charges to the bill, also marked up a similar amount.

A 3-page resume, then will bring you about $50, of which about $40 to $45 should be pure profit. If you think for a moment this is expensive, consider this: there are a number of executive consulting firms that do nothing more than this and will charge several thousands dollars to the client. A major benefit the job seeker gets from this service, apart from the printed resumes he can send out, is the chance to speak to someone who is sympathetic and understanding of his fears, ambitions, and goals. He is glad to pay for this.

Harry Lustig's business has expanded to the point where he has had to add "counselors," and it now makes him an income of over $40,000 a year.

HOW TO BUILD YOUR WEALTH BASE

Here's What You Need.   All you really need is a typewriter and a quiet place to work. There is a fair amount of paper work involved in this business, so you should have a place where you can spread out without having your family disturb your papers.

You will also need some basic know-how of resume preparation, and a supply of sample resumes that you can copy for style and format. A particularly good source of information is the *Executive Recruitment Guide*—a short course in effective resume preparation together with a list of several hundred high-level recruitment firms that solicit resumes from job-seekers. It is regularly up-dated and is available for $10 from James Peter Associates, Box 571, Westwood, New Jersey 07675.

How to Get Started.   This is not the best business to start out with friends as your first clients, notwithstanding the experience of Harry mentioned before. You will have to get some confidential information from your clients. If they are friends, they might be reluctant to tell you why they are looking for another job, what their past income history has been, and other details.

Your best bet in attracting clients is to run some ads in your local newspaper in the classified columns. Try to get space near the "help wanted" section, because job seekers will more likely see your ad there. This business is akin to other professional services, and aggressive advertising is usually frowned upon.

How to Promote.   The classified pages will help you most in the beginning. After you've gained some experience and stature, consider giving some talks to local business and fraternal groups on the subject of resume preparation and interviewing.

Use the secret trick known to every good consultant-speaker. Tell your listeners just enough to get them interested, but not enough to give away any real professional secrets or know-how. People will get interested, but then find they have to call on the expert to get the job done right.

Your Opportunity for Growth.   This business can bring great rewards for a person with a full-time job and no intention of going full time. Or, it can be used as a first step toward building your own employment counseling business, or even an employment agency.

Depending on how you work, you may or may not need a state license if you decide to open an agency. Check with your state employment office to be sure. Fortunes have been made in this business.

If you find that you enjoy the creative aspects of resume preparation, you should look into the opportunity offered by writing short paragraphs, as we have described it in this book. You might also offer a typing service to fill in the "lulls" in resume writing.

SCREEN AND STORM WINDOW SERVICE

Profits as Regular as the Seasons

Your Opportunity for Profit. Except in the warmer parts of the country, most homeowners have storm windows to replace the screens when cold weather comes. This means working with ladders and lugging screens and storm windows up and down. Most homeowners dread this job. If they can afford it, many will take the easy way out and replace these separate units with aluminum combination windows which are quickly changed with the seasons.

Yet, there are many homes without combination windows and someone must do the changing. You can be that person. Not only is this a service that is immediately attractive (and profitable to you) but it also provides a valuable introduction to your other services.

What You Can Earn. This business is strictly an hourly rate job. We've given you some pointers on figuring a fair hourly rate for yourself. Apply them here. Cleaning the windows is invariably included as part of the service and will add some hours to the job.

Thirty dollars is probably what you can average per house, and you can do perhaps two such houses a day. A helper will save you time and easily pay for himself in the extra work you can handle.

More important, this business is a good introduction to other services you can add. The general home cleaning business is one that comes to mind. So, too, are such businesses as attic and cellar hauling, air conditioner installation and removal (the seasons coincide), and lawn maintenance.

Once you free a homeowner of a burdensome job, he'll become your best salesman and will look around his house for other jobs you can tackle. You can call on a home twice a year and easily do $50 worth of work each time. That's $100 per customer per year.

You can certainly handle 50 customers a year in your spare time
—and earn $5,000 a year doing this.

HOW TO BUILD YOUR WEALTH BASE

Here's What You Need.   If you intend to stick to storm window
and screen services, the only tools you will need are a screwdriver
and a good extension ladder. You will almost certainly want to
add the window washing service with this, so provide yourself with
rags, chamois and a professional-quality squeegee for the windows.

How to Get Started.   On several occasions, we've told you to
cruise neighborhoods looking for likely prospects. A quick look at
the houses you pass will quickly tell you which homes have the
kind of windows that need to be changed with the seasons.

How to Promote.   The best promotion gimmick here is the curb
stenciling service that is described elsewhere in this book. Refer to
that section for the secret of attracting a customer to your service.

If you don't want to try that approach, then you can use a simple postcard mailing to the homeowners you've spotted on your
travels. The classified columns of your newspaper are a good
source of business, because they usually have headings for a variety of home cleaning and maintenance services.

Your Opportunity for Growth.   Grow by doing these three
things:

1. Concentrate on getting regular, twice-a-year customers.
   This will cut down on the time and expense of finding new
   customers.
2. Try to sell each customer a "package" of services tailored
   to his needs. For example; twice a year, you will put up
   and take down the screens and storm windows, clean the
   outside windows, repair storm damage and fertilize the
   lawn in the spring, and seed and mulch in the fall. It's surprising how quickly the jobs add up to a healthy profit for
   you.
3. When the work gets too much for you to handle by yourself, look for reliable outside help, and concentrate on the
   business details of your growing home service business.

SEALING DRIVEWAYS

Smooth the Way to Profits

Your Opportunity for Profit. If you were to check with your local Better Business Bureau, you'd find that one of the most common frauds is the old story of the traveling "driveway sealers."

For protection and long life, a blacktop driveway should be given a coat of special driveway sealer every year. These fast-buck operators travel about a neighborhood, and give the homeowner a story about how they have just finished a job in the neighborhood and have some material "left over." They will be glad to do the driveway at a low price.

Once the homeowner says yes, he's in for a surprise. The material is inferior and sometimes takes forever to dry. The itinerant driveway sealers have their money and are nowhere to be found.

Should this sorry experience discourage you? Actually, it can be one of your strongest selling points. The fact that numbers of homeowners fall for this story shows how easy it is to "sell" the idea of driveway sealing. The fact that you use approved materials, guarantee your work, and are located in town can be of enormous advantage to you in the promotion of your service.

What You Can Earn. Prices of materials vary. You'll be smart to use the best available, because, in the long run, it will do the best job. A good strong starting point is to estimate the quantity of sealer needed and double the cost for your price to the homeowner. If the driveway presents special problems like patching or extensive cleaning, you'll have to raise the basic figure. An average 40 foot driveway should bring you $30 to $50, depending on how wide it is.

HOW TO BUILD YOUR WEALTH BASE

Here's What You Need.   Sealing a driveway requires very few
tools. Bring your own hose for cleaning the driveway of debris just
in case the customer has a built-in sprinkling system.

A combination brush and squeegee and some cans of good
sealer are all you need. If you intend to do patching, then you'll
need several bags of "instant" patching material and a tamper to
smooth it down. Even with the water-base materials, the job can
get messy. If you don't have use of a small truck to carry your materials, be sure to protect the trunk of your car with a layer of plastic sheeting.

How to Get Started.   Start by taking a slow cruise around your
neighborhood. Notice how many driveways you see that are in
need of sealing to prevent winter frost damage. In particular, note
the driveways that have just been sealed by some ambitious homeowner. The houses on both sides of his are very likely prospects
because the homeowner is probably talking-up the advantages of
sealing to them.

How to Promote.   With this list of prospects, you can get to
work preparing a simple postcard announcement or even a hand-
written note to mail to them. Tell about your service and give
them an idea of what it will cost. Above all, mention the advantage of working with *you,* a local businessman who is located in
town, and who stands ready to guarantee his work.

If you don't get a response to the cards, follow them up with
phone calls in the evening, when the man of the house will be
home. This two-step promotion technique can result in an unusu-
ally high percentage of sales.

Your Opportunity for Growth.   Sealing a driveway is such a
simply learned task that any ambitious teen-ager can do a very
creditable job. Find one in your family, or among friends, and you
can take on twice as many jobs.

This is an ideal opportunity to add to any of the other "outdoor" type businesses described in this book.

SEWING INSTRUCTION AND PATTERN ALTERATION

Stitch Up Profits

Your Opportunity for Profit. In the last few years, the sales of material and patterns for home sewing has increased many-fold. According to all projections, this trend will continue, which means that if you are fast with a needle, and able to explain what you are doing in a simple manner, you can make a lot of money as the "home sewing consultant."

Most women can handle the routine sewing jobs, but when it comes to making anything more elaborate than a shift, they're in trouble. If you have the talent—even many men have it—you can teach people to sew, and show them how to alter patterns. The altering of patterns immediately establishes you as the sewing expert for people who are planning to diet, but are in the process of making something to their present measurements.

Carolyn Weber made all her own clothes ever since she was a child. Of course, she was the envy of her neighbors, who wished they could make beautiful clothes at a fraction of what they would cost in a store. One day, a friend offered to pay her to alter a pattern, and she has been in business ever since. Some people call her a "sew and sew," but Carolyn laughs all the way to the bank.

What You Can Earn. There are three ways to make money here: Instruction in basic and advanced sewing techniques, pattern alteration, and doing the actual sewing work for others. Perhaps you will do all three, but the charges should be the same for the first two only. Three to five dollars an hour should be the range for teaching and altering. Mrs. Weber, who works at this business about 3 days a week can make over $8,000 a year for pleasant, part-time activity.

When you actually do the work of producing a finished garment for someone, you should charge considerably more. In fact, your charges should be at least half again as much as a store would charge for a similar product, ready-made. After all, this is now a custom-tailored garment. Be sure to sew in some identification of yours. Small embroidered initials, or even labels that you can have made. Check the sewing magazines for a label source.

HOW TO BUILD YOUR WEALTH BASE

Here's What You Need.   If you are only an average seamstress, you had better steer clear of this business. If you have the talent, the only other thing you'll need is a sewing machine, and the usual accessories so familiar to you: pattern tracing wheel, scissors, needles, pins, thread, and whatever else you might have found helpful. A portable machine is often an asset, because you can visit your students, or give demonstrations at club meetings.

How to Get Started.   Show off clothes you have made. Do it at club meetings, parties and other gatherings. Then, announce to your friends that you are offering a home "sewing consulting" service. Be sure to tell them the price, and offer discounts for group projects. Ten percent for 10 or more students is about right.

How to Promote.   Beyond the word-of-mouth approach already discussed, the best tactics often include bulletin board announce-ments at your church, or social club, and an occasional classified ad in local newspapers when the seasons change. You might try to get the local chapter of Weight Watchers to throw some pattern alteration business your way.

Your Opportunity for Growth.   Obviously, the best way to grow in this business is to have larger attendance at group sessions. Be-cause you can do only so much, larger classes represent the ex-penditure of the same energy, but for a greater pay. Try to get your program on the bill at the local adult school. Give it a twist like, "Sewing for Men," or "What to Do Until the Price of Clothes Comes Down."

You might consider a simple "franchise" operation in which you set up other equally talented people in other towns to use your "methods."

Keep the local newspaper editors informed. This sort of activity is always good "copy."

SHOPPING SERVICES

You Deliver a Profit to Yourself

Your Opportunity for Profit.   It wasn't too long ago that stores, supermarkets included, would send a man to take your order, and then deliver it for no more than the cost of the groceries involved. But, as business became less and less personal, this convenience disappeared.

The service is gone, but the need is still alive. Here is a neat little opportunity for working on your Wealth Base while you do your own shopping.

Consider the needs of the shut-in, the working wife, or the person too busy to spend much time shopping. Not only food shopping, but all the other essential errands in keeping a household together. These people, and there are many of them, are prime prospects for custom shopping services and other errands at nominal cost.

What You Can Earn.   This service can be priced in several ways. You can charge a flat percentage of the total price of the completed order—with a 10% surcharge about the tops that can be asked. Or, you can charge by the trip, the charge depending on the amount of time it takes to do the job.

Once you get a string of regular customers, you can get very efficient in handling a number of customers on a single shopping trip. Even a nominal charge per customer—say 2 dollars—can earn you 10 dollars for a morning's work.

HOW TO BUILD YOUR WEALTH BASE

Here's What You Need. You will almost certainly need a car, since you will be featuring door-to-door service to your customers. The one personal characteristic you'll need is persistence, and enjoyment in shopping and tracking down bargains.

How to Get Started. Look for a concentration of potential customers. Apartment families are often working families, with little time for shopping. Such families are concentrated in an apartment house—making your job of contacting them so much easier. Visit apartments in your area and ring doorbells. Your best prospects probably won't answer. They are the working families most likely to need your service.

Be sure to have a supply of simple announcements that you can slip under these doors. Ask the superintendent if you can post an announcement in the laundry room. Most important—be sure to check with your local clergymen. They are a prime source of news about shut-ins needing the kind of help you are offering.

How to Promote. Direct contact, word-of-mouth, and some little direct mail are about the best ways of getting things going. The direct-mail can as simple as a hand-written post-card mailed to all the prospects in a near-by apartment house or senior citizens community. Follow up by phone a few days later.

The stores you shop in should be most pleased to promote your service. After all, you'll be doing some heavy buying from them. Talk to the store owner or manager. He might even let you put a small announcement near the check-out counter in his store.

Your Opportunity for Growth. You spend valuable time doing your own shopping. Why not use the same time to work on your own Wealth Base? That's the beauty of this little business. If, after a time, you want to expand this service, consider adding assistants to your staff. They will do the same thing you started out doing—shopping and delivering orders. You spend your time on the development of new business.

You might consider expanding your business along more sophisticated lines. People who are interested in antiques, rare books, bits of Americana or items of nostalgia, are generally willing to pay well if you are successful in seeking out some items they are looking for. The secret here is to build a large "want list" from various potential buyers. At best, you will be successful in finding only a few of the items in a reasonable time.

If you've taken on additional businesses, such as attic and celler hauling, and perhaps the custom lamp making business, you will have a group of related enterprises each helping the other to build your Wealth Base.

SIGN MAKING

Show and Sell

Your Opportunity for Profit. Keep your eyes open the next time you walk through a business district, a public building, or any institution which has people coming and going throughout the day. You'll be amazed at the number and variety of signs. While many signs are permanent in metal or paint, many are temporary notices of one sort or another that are usually made by hand.

A store announces some special sale . . . a bank wants to tell about some new service . . . or a local fraternal group tries to spread the word about its annual fund-raising dance. These are just a few of the many times where a sign, a poster, or banner is needed to tell the public the news.

Making these signs can be a lucrative part-time business for someone in town, particularly if he has an even slight feel for lettering.

What You Can Earn. You will be charging for your time, plus whatever materials are involved. Your promotion and materials will cost you next to nothing, so just about everything you take in is pure profit. If an average sign uses a quarter's worth of materials, it's a lot. And a sign like that is probably worth at least a couple of dollars, depending on the amount of time it took to make it. Some sign makers charge by the word, and a dollar a word is not uncommon.

HOW TO BUILD YOUR WEALTH BASE

Here's What You Need.   Ideally, you should have some talent, or experience with simple art materials. This doesn't mean that you have to be an artist in order to make money in this business. Most signs consist of fairly simple designs and lettering. Even the lettering can be done with stencils.

If you have doubts, then visit the book rack of the art store in which you plan to purchase your starter materials of poster boards and paints. Innumerable low-cost, soft-cover books are available on the techniques of sign painting. These will show you how to use illustrations.

How to Promote.   Your first job should be for yourself. Make some simple signs with your name and phone number, and place them in strategic spots. The bulletin boards of various churches, fraternal organizations, and other public locations are good places to start.

Visit the owners or managers of local stores, banks, markets, and other businesses. With a sample case of several different signs, you can usually walk away with at least a sample order. Remember, you will seldom make money on the first order where you have to spend time showing the potential customer what you can do and explaining your prices. The real money comes later with the easy, repeat business from satisfied customers.

Finally, get yourself some distinctive "logo" as advertising men call it. This is your emblem and should include your name, address, phone number and a few words about your business. Spend a few dollars to have this made into a rubber stamp and you can include it on the bottom of every sign you make without having to hand-draw it each time.

How to Get Started.   Your first job is to size up the market and know where to spend your time drumming up business. In your normal day-to-day activities, keep an eye out for signs, or the *need* for signs. Sometimes, the greatest potential is in the unlikeliest place.

A young man attending a midwestern college earned a good part of his tuition by making signs. Every fraternity and school organization had one or more signs made sometime during a semester to announce some function. Seldom did a week go by when he didn't have one or two fairly large jobs waiting for him.

Your Opportunity for Growth. You will reach a point where you can't earn more money by taking on more jobs, simply because you haven't that much free time available. By this time, you should have built up a following among sign users so that they will come to you automatically. You can, therefore, think of adding a capable assistant. Again, here is an ideal opportunity for a man and wife team, where each contributes his or her own special talents to the enterprise.

SILK SCREEN PRINTING

Yesterday's Craft for Today's Profits

Your Opportunity for Profit. What would you say if someone told you that you could produce hundreds of museum quality prints, posters, or even intricate works of art, in full color, on equipment no more complicated or expensive than a few yards of cloth stretched on a simple frame, some paints, and a squeegee?

It sounds too good to be true, but it is, and it's called silk screen printing. The process produces high-quality "printing" in as many colors as you wish. You can, if you're talented, produce original works of art. However, you don't need great artistic abilities to turn out posters, signs, and other printed messages impossible or prohibitively expensive to turn out on commercial printing presses.

What You Can Earn.   Your earnings here depend on what kind of silk screen printing you may be doing. You can turn out 500 posters in a single weekend and easily charge $250 for the job. The process is particularly adapted to printing on cloth. If you decorate tablecloths, neckties, or handbags, the price of the item can usually be doubled over that of an undecorated item. A plain $3 tie is now worth $6; a $7 tablecloth is now worth $15; and so on.

HOW TO BUILD YOUR WEALTH BASE

Here's What You Need.   You will need the basic equipment and materials of silk-screen printing. Fortunately, these are not expensive at all. Silk-screen printing is really a stencil process. A piece of high-quality silk is stretched over a simple wooden frame. A stencil is glued to the underside of the silk with cutouts representing the areas that you want to print. This screen is laid over a piece of paper, some paint is put in the frame, and it is squeegeed through the openings onto the paper beneath. Lift up the screen, and you have a printed sheet of paper. If you want additional colors, you put the printed paper thru other stencil frames with other colors.

A lot of variations in printing, stenciling, and choice of inks is possible. Yet, a complete outfit that will let you tackle high-quality work in many colors, should cost you between $50 and $100 and be compact enough to store in a closet.

If you've never done silk-screen printing, ask your librarian to show you some of the many craft books available on this subject. Better still, enroll in an art course if one is available and learn it from a teacher.

How to Get Started.   Once you've practiced the craft for a while, dozens of profitable opportunities for using it will suggest themselves to you. Basically, you are in the specialty printing business. Anything out of the ordinary that a commercial printer would balk at, is a potential sales opportunity for you. You can print on paper, cloth, metal, wood, even curved pieces of furniture if necessary. Start by looking around and listing all the items and places where this type of printing can be used. You'll be amazed!

How to Promote.   The specialized nature of this craft lends itself well to word of mouth advertising. Anyone you come in contact with is usually so impressed with the results that he spreads the word around. There won't be an event or happening in town, but someone will want you to run off several dozen posters announcing the event.

Gift shops are ideal to cultivate. Team up with someone who can produce trays, plaques, and bases, and you'll have a steady market for these same items now decorated with silk-screen printing. Simple bolts of cloth can be decorated and resold at handsome profits through quality fabric shops in town. On a mundane level, you can stencil print team names on uniforms, produce political banners, and do dozens of jobs that are impossible to run through a regular printing press.

Most of your promoting will be direct contacts with outlets like gift shops. If you want to do items like banners and posters, then take some space in the classified pages of your telephone directory. This is the sort of specialized service that people look to a directory first for information.

Your Opportunity for Growth.   This business can grow into a large, full-time operation. It all depends on how much time and work you want to invest. On a larger scale, you'll have to invest in semi-automatic machines, photographic stencil making equipment, and other tools to handle all kinds of jobs on the most economical basis.

As a "basement business," however, you can keep mighty busy, and still have the satisfaction of seeing substantial profit dollars roll in.

SMALL APPLIANCE REPAIR

Fix Your Weak Bankbook Fast

Your Opportunity for Profit. If you could survey the country to find out what is the most needed service, chances are it would be this business—small appliance repair. There must be millions of toasters, coffee pots, vacuums, fans, and other appliances junked each day because the owners could not find someone to repair them. Factory service centers are usually so jammed with work that waiting six weeks for a simple repair job is not at all unusual.

Small appliance repair can be quickly learned by anyone with any intelligence at all, and a liking for working with one's hands. Surprisingly enough, you'll find that once you've gotten some experience, you'll be able to spot troubles quickly, because the basic appliances all work on similar principles.

What You Can Earn. You charge for the parts you use at retail prices (even though you buy them at the wholesale price) and for the time it takes you to do the job. You should earn anywhere from $4 to $8 an hour clear profit on your time. The work is easy, can be done with little investment in tools or space. And, it's ideal for part-time work.

It's not uncommon to pull in $8,000 to $10,000 a year, working only 20 hours or so a week.

HOW TO BUILD YOUR WEALTH BASE

Here's What You Need. You will need some training or experience in the repair of simple home appliances. The best suggestion we can give is that you investigate some of the books available on this subject. If you're serious about making this a full-time business (and it can be a very secure and profitable one) then you should explore the offerings of correspondence schools in this area.

Tools for this business are not very complicated or expensive, either. Screwdrivers, pliers, soldering iron, wrenches, and a continuity tester will see you through most jobs. Spare parts are available from service centers, manufacturers, and from scrapped appliances. Although you may think that every model of an appliance is different, you'll quickly discover that the differences are mostly in external design. The "insides" are quite similar.

How to Get Started.   Start by collecting all the discarded and non-working appliances you can find. This is the best way to gain experience, and to build an inventory of parts. Don't worry if the items are old. Remember, most of the time someone will want you to repair an older appliance, and you might just have the needed part that can be cannibalized from an old coffee maker or electric fan that might be in your stock.

How to Promote.   Word of mouth advertising will work swiftly here. If word gets around that you provide fast, reliable service, you'll quickly find yourself with quite a bit of work waiting for you. Advertising in your phone directory will also pay off.

Your Opportunity for Growth.   Don't make the mistake of growing so fast that *your* customers will have to wait six weeks or more for a simple repair. Then, you're no better than the service center that irked your customers originally. Rather, turn away work honestly; better yet, train someone to help you. Not too surprising is the fact that this work is easily learned by women. In fact, because they have patience and a delicate touch, some repairs are better handled by women. Train your wife as your number one helper and keep all the profits in the family!

SMALL ITEM WELDING

Put Together a Neat Income for Yourself

Your Opportunity for Profit.   Did you ever break something around the house or garage that could be quickly put back into service if only you had a welder? A welder is a rare tool for a home handyman, and regular welding shops are often reluctant to take on small jobs.

Investing in a small welder can funnel a lot of this business your way. Not only will the machine pay for itself, but you'll earn profits on it year after year. When added to the profits you can earn in related businesses, the total can add up nicely as a part-time income.

What You Can Earn.   Only after you've used a welder for a little time will you be able to estimate the amount of time a job will take and how much you should charge for the repair. Be guided by these pointers:

1. Your time is worthwhile. Make sure you price it fairly and that you recover the cost of your materials, plus a profit for your efforts. Ten dollars an hour is not unreasonable when you consider this includes the wear and tear on your welder.
2. Some jobs would take too long to fix considering the value of the article or the cost of replacing it with a new one. Make sure your customer is aware of this before you begin.

In a rural area, where farmers are constantly in need of welding services to keep their equipment in shape (teeth and blades break frequently) you can earn a substantial income—several hundred dollars a week during the busy season is entirely possible. In suburban areas, broken toys, bikes, and home tools will keep you busy.

HOW TO BUILD YOUR WEALTH BASE

Here's What You Need. An electric welder, or arc welder should probably be your first choice. You can add gas welding later on if the need appears. If your home is wired to take an electric stove or clothes dryer, you should have no problem in using an electric welder.

First look for used machines. Since there are few moving parts to wear out, a used welder will give as good service as a new one. A small, but adequate welder can be picked up for a hundred dollars or so. There are very inexpensive, hobbyist-quality machines that are sold by mail. They will work in their limited way, but you'll probably be better off buying a larger machine right from the start.

How to Get Started. Practice on your own jobs as a start. In a short time, word will get around that you have a welder and neighbors will be asking you to do some jobs for them. These first jobs can be a very effective form of advertising for you.

Before you get too deep into the business, check with your local fire chief. Even though an electric welder is relatively safe, there are sometimes local ordinances that have to be observed, particularly if you make money with the operation.

How to Promote. Phone directory advertising is good for a business of this type. So too, is a sign if you live in an area where that would be permitted. People need welding services only when something breaks and will remember a name if they see it frequently in their travels about town.

Your Opportunity for Growth. This is a good part-time opportunity; but, unless you see yourself opening a full-service welding shop, you should think of adding other services to your line. You'll be dealing with people who need various fixing services around the house. Consider some of the other businesses we speak about in these pages. These are particularly suitable, since your advertising can sell all the services at the same time:

(1) Spray painting, (2) Lawn mower maintenance, (3) Grinding and sharpening services, (4) Preparation work for home painters.

SMALL MOTOR REPAIR AND MAINTENANCE

Small Motors Turn Over Big Profits

Your Opportunity for Profit. A good motor mechanic for your car is tough to find. Even tougher to find is someone to service the small motors in lawn mowers, outboards, mini-bikes, snow-mobiles, and the like. Think how fast the need is growing. A few years ago, both trail-bikes and snow-mobiles were virtually unknown. Today, they are a booming hobby.

By concentrating on small motors, you can build up a very lucrative full or part-time business in very short order. Winter and summer, there is some machine with a motor needing service. In summer, it's lawnmowers and sweepers; in winter, it's snowblowers or snow-mobiles. Because most of these motors are similar, you can repair virtually all of them without a lot of training or experience. Another advantage is that your stock of parts can be kept at a minimum because many are interchangeable.

What You Can Earn. You make money on parts and the labor involved. Together, you should be able to earn a hefty $10 to $15 an hour clear profit. Multiply that by the number of hours you can spend, and you'll quickly see what kind of opportunity we are discussing here. A spare-time income of $150 a week, or $6000 to $8000 a year is not unlikely once you acquire some word-of-mouth reputation.

HOW TO BUILD YOUR WEALTH BASE

Here's What You Need. Small motors are not hard to find; they are being junked all the time. Lay your hands on as many as you can if you need experience with different types. You may not get them to work, but at least you'll discover why they won't work. Special tools for working on small motors are available in auto-supply stores, and through the large mail-order houses.

Information on servicing the motors is easy to find. Articles appear regularly in the various handyman magazines; books are available at your library; and service manuals can be obtained from the manufacturers.

Another advantage of working with small motors is the fact that you don't need much room to work on them.

How to Get Started. You will need a modest amount of space to set up your shop. A basement can be used, but a separate building (like a garage) is preferable because you will be starting gasoline engines and noise and ventilation problems are solved more easily in an outdoor location.

How to Promote. A variety of promotion techniques can be used with this business. Strive to get a mix of both wholesale and retail business. Wholesale business is the repair work you do for dealers who sell the various machines. Retail business is the business you do directly with the owner. Call on the dealers in your area for wholesale business; advertise in your telephone directory and newspaper classified section to attract retail business.

Most small motors need regular maintenance. Few owners remember this fact and usually wait until the motor quits completely. Capitalize on this fact by maintaining a careful list of all your customers. At regular intervals, appropriate to the season and machine he may own, send the owner a reminder to bring in his mower or snowblower, or whatever, for a maintenance check.

Your Opportunity for Growth. This is one business that can quickly grow into a profitable full-time shop. Remember one thing: your business will prosper only to the degree that you can provide fast, reliable service. A full-time shop invariably means training some helpers to help out with the work.

SPECIAL MESSENGER SERVICE

This Business Delivers Profits

Your Opportunity for Profit. When you think of a messenger service, the first thing that comes to mind is delivering packages for stores, and it's not a very bright picture. But, consider that there are many businesses which urgently need someone to do their delivery work; and that their deliveries are often small envelopes which do not require the investment in a truck. Specifically, here are some businesses which constantly seek good delivery facilities:

- Printers—for rush proofs and copy, not for large shipments of finished printing
- Advertising agencies—for proofs, copy, and artwork
- Engineers and architects—for blueprints and drawings
- Art studios—for artwork, layouts and proofs
- Typographers—not for heavy type, but printed "repros" of printed matter
- Any business with near-by branch offices which must exchange paperwork: banks, stores, accountants, etc.

The one thing all of these businesses have in common is that they require prompt, reliable delivery. Most messenger services that handle parcels cannot guarantee the kind of service required. But you can, as a specialist in prompt delivery of critical paperwork.

What You Can Earn.   The best way to make big money in this business is to line up several companies for a regular schedule of pick-ups and deliveries. This way you guarantee your weekly income, and don't have to depend on any of the seasonal and business fluctuations.

For example: advertising agencies and art studios are in constant need of people to deliver copy, art, and layouts, most of which are paper envelopes. If the agency account executive has to handle the routine of such delivery, his time becomes very expensive to the agency. But, as the specialist, you could handle half a dozen agencies, art studios, typographers within a 10 mile radius, and charge each a flat rate of $50 a week, for a minimum of 3 stops a day. Because all of the businesses are related, you will often make one stop for several of the businesses, saving considerable time.

Bruce Carleton, a retired bus driver, did just this, and with five companies on a regular schedule, he grosses $250 a week, works about 6 hours a day, and is very pleased with his retirement income. Including special trips, beyond his contract, Bruce grossed better than $15,000 in his second year—far greater than his salary when he worked full time.

HOW TO BUILD YOUR WEALTH BASE

Here's What You Need.   All you need is a reliable car. You should consider the availability of a back-up vehicle, even if it is only the car of a friend, should your car be out of service.

Check your insurance. Your car is now being used for business, and the policy should be re-written to cover it. Also, see if your state or town has any special licensing requirements. Most states require special licenses to carry people, but very few have any regulations, other than basic insurance for a delivery service.

How to Get Started.   Once you have checked up on insurance and licensing, simply go to the yellow pages, and make a list of the businesses mentioned earlier. Then, use the direct approach. Visit each one, and tell them of your plans. This will get you business in a hurry.

How to Promote.   Advertising is an expense you can afford after you have a few regular customers. Running ads will be a slow way to get business, so don't depend too heavily on it. You'll find that most of your business will come from referrals from satisfied customers. For this reason, make sure that you perform as promised.

Your Opportunity for Growth.   Obviously, you can expand to the limit of time you have as an individual, then you must add people. You can add people who have cars, and pay them for their work, plus an allowance for the car—10¢ a mile is common—or you can buy additional cars and simply hire people to drive them over the routes you have established. Either way, you will find that expansion will be costly, and others who have started similar businesses have been content to run their own routes without the headaches of other drivers. This business is a natural to add to the advertising distribution service described elsewhere in the book. It can also be added conveniently to the private transportation service, also described in this book.

SPOT FINISHING

A Vanishing Art Can Bring Steady Profits

Your Opportunity for Profit.   For every piece of furniture that is completely refinished, there must be a thousand pieces that need only touch-up finishing to repair some damage. Cigarette burns, rings from wet glasses, dents, scratches, and other mars to the finish of a piece of furniture can be removed or repaired with a technique known as "spot finishing."

For some reason, spot finishers get more and more rare each year; yet the need for them is growing by leaps and bounds. As our society gets more mobile, more and more people move each year. And who has moved without some damage to a coffee table, dresser, or valued chair? A good spot finisher can earn good money repairing such damage—and *the insurance company pays the bill.*

If you have some skill in working with tools and finishes, you should certainly add this skill to your background. Some practice will be necessary, especially since matching colors can be fussy, but once the skill is acquired, you can always turn it into dollars without any selling at all.

What You Can Earn.   A furniture store unpacks a $400 dresser and discovers a two-inch scratch made by a careless use of an un-crating tool. You can render this scratch absolutely invisible in half an hour and easily charge $10 for the job. A housewife is horrified to discover ugly white rings on her expensive end tables the morning after a party. An hour's work will remove the rings and make you $25 richer.

These and other examples suggest the kind of money waiting to be made in this business. The work from a single furniture store can fill your spare time hours if you wish and earn you $100 a week and more.

HOW TO BUILD YOUR WEALTH BASE

Here's What You Need. The background skill has already been touched upon. The actual tools and materials are relatively inexpensive and can be obtained from mail-order houses that advertise in hobby and woodworking magazines. A typical kit will include "French" polish and polishing pads, an assortment of colored shellac sticks for filling gouges and dents, and an assortment of knives.

To these special items, you will need some ordinary woodworking tools to repair a loose rung on a chair, or to glue down a chipped piece of veneer.

How to Get Started. If a course is being offered in this subject at your local vocational school, by all means try to attend. Some good books are available on the subject which your librarian can locate for you. As far as finding practice pieces, you probably have them in your own living room.

How to Promote. The easiest place to find jobs is at your local furniture store. They deliver dozens of pieces of expensive furniture every day. And every day some customers call who have "discovered" a scratch or mar that occurred in shipment. The more expensive the piece, the more the likelihood of a complaint.

The store could take the piece back and replace it. However, it is much simpler to send a man to spot finish the item in the customer's home. You can get these jobs by simply telling the store manager of your business and showing him samples of your work, if necessary.

Get in touch with your insurance agents and moving companies because they are constantly exposed to claims of furniture damage. Again, they will many times hire you to go to a client's home and repair the damage, and then accept your bill for the work performed.

Finally, you might want to take on "retail" business yourself.

The best way to advertise your business is in the telephone directory under the heading of "furniture-repair and restoration."

Your Opportunity for Growth.   Like all skill businesses, this business is pretty much a one-man affair, but you can train an assistant to do the simpler jobs. A better thought is to make this service part of a larger business devoted to furniture repair, antique restoration and refinishing. It is surprising how a relatively small area will support a substantial business in this field.

SPRAY PAINTING

Paint a Profit Picture for Yourself

Your Opportunity for Profit.   Did you ever try to paint a louvred door . . . a rough board fence . . . or something similar with a paintbrush? You waste an awful lot of paint and use up a great deal of patience in doing the job. And then, it doesn't look as good as you hoped. Next time, you promise yourself, you'll get a paint sprayer.

Every homeowner has faced this thought, but few of them ever invest in a paint sprayer. Once the job is done, they forget about it until the next time they need it. If you invested in a paint sprayer, not only could you do all those pesky jobs for yourself, but you could also recover the cost of the equipment on the next few jobs you tackle. After that, you'd be making pure profit on every job you do.

What You Can Earn.   If you invest in fairly large capacity equipment, you can take on house painting jobs. If you want to get into the house-painting business, then go after equipment of this sort. Remember this, however: spray painting is usually done on the exterior of buildings. Outside painting isn't a very practical part-time business, unless you have long weekends to work. Obviously, you can't paint houses at night in your spare time.

But—you can paint toys, doors, and furniture in your spare time, any time! Fix up a corner of the garage or basement as a spraying area, and you'll find a variety of jobs to keep your equipment busy.

This service is similar to small item welding as far as charges go, and you should refer to that business for more details. In fact, spray painting and small item welding go together well as businesses because you are providing needed repair and maintenance services to the same type of customer.

HOW TO BUILD YOUR WEALTH BASE

Here's What You Need. You will need a paint spraying outfit. There are some very small, inexpensive, self-contained units that are adequate for spraying watery liquids like insecticides and thin stains. They simply can't handle paint of any body, and you should avoid them.

Instead, check the catalogs of the large mail-order houses for spray paint outfits. An adequate one can be purchased (many times second-hand) for $100 or so. Heavy duty outfits for outside painters cost much more. Get an outfit that will permit you to use both suction and pressure feeds so you can handle a variety of work.

How to Get Started. Basically, you're offering a specialized painting service. Most of your work will probably be no larger than a piece of furniture. Set up a clean corner in which to work and make sure it is properly ventilated. If you plan on using lacquers, the simplest thing to do is to plan on working outdoors on a still day. If you must work indoors, you'll need plenty of forced ventilation with volatile finishes.

How to Promote. Everybody needs something spray painted at one time or another. Once you let the word around the neighborhood that you own the equipment, you'll find inquiries coming to you. This, plus something in the classified section of your phone directory, will be your best source of business.

Your Opportunity for Growth. Check the opportunities listed under small-item welding for suggestions on how this business can be expanded. You can also consider adding it to the business of antique refinishing, spot finishing, and as something in your tool exchange business.

SURVEY INTERVIEWING

Get Paid for Talking

Your Opportunity for Profit.   Government agencies and businesses spend over a half a billion dollars every year just to find out what people think. With this kind of money being spent, it is imperative that they get the answers they need. If you like to talk to people, you can not only make money, but you can have fun doing it.

Interviewers can handle their assignments on the phone, by calling door-to-door, by visiting local stores, and by specific assignment to important decision makers. Any way it is handled, it is a fascinating and profitable business.

Mrs. Lois Frost was called on by an interviewer, and while being interviewed, she was impressed with the prospect of doing this kind of work herself. The interviewer recommended a special course given through the mail, and soon she was on her way to making over $12,000 a year, from a converted sun porch in her home.

What You Can Earn.   Interviewers are usually paid by the number of calls they make. Because the amount of probing required by each assignment varies, it is impossible to give exact figures of what can be made per call. But, many people have made well over $100 a week in spare time interviewing assignments. Of course, one of the benefits of this business is that you must maintain some form of home office, even if it's only a corner of a room . . . and that's a tax deduction.

HOW TO BUILD YOUR WEALTH BASE

Here's What You Need. You don't need any experience, although you should be at ease talking with all kinds of people. There are two good ways to break into this lucrative field:

- Seek free training and beginner assignments from local research agencies. Check the yellow pages for market research and advertising agencies in your area, and give them a call.
- Seek some training through such organizations as the Universal School in Dallas, Texas. Send for their bulletin to 6801 Hillcrest Ave., Dallas, Texas 75205.

How to Get Started. Once you feel comfortable handling an interview, you can either contact manufacturers in your area directly, or continue to work through the research agencies. For part time work, this is the best bet. We'll tell you how to become a "research contractor" when we talk about growth.

How to Promote. If you are simply taking assignment from agencies and manufacturers, the only thing you can do is to keep after them with letters and phone calls.

Your Opportunity for Growth. Here's the kicker: you can only make so much money doing the interviews yourself, and there are just so many hours in a day. You should consider becoming the "contractor." As such, you train a staff of people to do the interviewing, and then offer this trained group to the manufacturers and agencies. Obviously, you should plan to open branches in other towns as soon as it becomes possible.

TINWARE STENCILING AND DECORATING

It's Easy to Paint a Profit Picture

Your Opportunity for Profit.   Painting and stenciling tinware is a popular hobby that you can turn into a spare time income without much investment. The techniques of stripping borders and using colored powders to create pictures are similar to those used to decorate painted pieces of furniture. In fact, this is a good skill to add to a business involving antique restoration and spot finishing.

You can earn money in several ways once you've acquired some skill:

1. Restoring old pieces, either tinware, tole ware, or painted furniture.
2. Creating new pieces that you can sell through gift and consignment shops.
3. Giving lessons to private individuals or groups. This last can be the most profitable in terms of what you can earn for an hour of your time.

What You Can Earn.   We've mentioned in other places how to charge for things you sell, and for your time in repairing or restoring antiques. Giving lessons to groups can provide you with an impressive income. You can get a group of 10 people enrolled in a class that will cover five sessions of two hours each. This means you spend ten hours actually teaching this class. Each person can be charged a minimum of $15 for the series of lessons—a very reasonable fee for almost personalized instruction. The class, therefore, earns you $150 for ten hours work—or $15 an hour.

By working with various women's groups in your locality, you can have classes going all the time, earning $150 a week or more for enjoyable work. Because a delicate touch is essential, this work seems particularly suitable for women. A husband and wife team can combine this business with that of antique refinishing, and really have a money-making business.

HOW TO BUILD YOUR WEALTH BASE

Here's What You Need.   You will need the basic skill in tinware painting and stenciling. If you can find a class nearby, by all means attend it to learn the fundamentals. Otherwise, you can pick up most of the help you need through various hobby magazines and books.

The materials are relatively inexpensive. Paint and varnish, various bronzing powders, a striping tool, and an assortment of fine brushes for detail work will carry you through nicely.

How to Get Started.   You will need a place you can call your studio and it should reflect the good taste of your products. A corner of this studio should be made dust-free with plastic drapes. To do quality work, you must avoid dust settling on painted or varnished pieces while they are drying.

How to Promote.   Your promotion techniques will depend a lot on the kind of business you're trying to generate. If you want to specialize in classes, then personal contact with as many likely groups as possible, will give you leads to follow up. Also, be sure to get in touch with the director of any adult education classes that may be run in your area once you've acquired some skill and reputation.

If you want to do actual work for profit, your best bet will be to call on owners of gift shops, antique shops, and other likely prospects. Because the technique is interesting to the general group of newspaper readers, you should find it fairly easy to get your local newspaper editor to run an illustrated feature story on your craft. Cultivate such contacts as much as possible—it's the best publicity you can get.

Your Opportunity for Growth.   Like so many other businesses we cover in this book, you can grow in this business in direct proportion to the time you want to invest in running it. Add this craft to others as has been suggested and you've soon built an enviable income either full or spare time.

TOY ASSEMBLY AND REPAIR

Work So Others May Play

Your Opportunity for Profit.   Visit a bike shop a few weeks before Christmas, or ask to speak to the manager of the toy department of a large store just after a big shipment has arrived for a forthcoming sale. In either case you'll see harried men, and the reason is not too hard to discover. Most bikes and larger toys— wagons and gym sets for example—must be assembled before they can be sold. Some discount houses leave the assembly to the final purchaser. But, the better shops have to spend time and money putting the merchandise in saleable shape.

Here's where a man with screwdriver and a few wrenches can make himself extra money with virtually no effort at soliciting the business. Like so many of the other businesses described in this book, this one won't make you rich overnight. What it will do, however, is put those extra dollars regularly in your pocket that are vital if you are ever to accumulate a Wealth Base that puts you on the road to something really big.

What You Can Earn.   Your best bet is to charge by the hour for your service in the beginning. After you've gotten the knack of assembling the common articles in short order, you can quote a flat price per piece—so much for a bike, etc. Your work should earn you $3 to $6 an hour, depending on how well and how fast you can work.

HOW TO BUILD YOUR WEALTH BASE

Here's What You Need.   You'll need nothing more than a few common tools and spare time. Any special tools will be supplied by your customer, and you will work at his location. You don't even need any space to work at home.

How to Get Started.   Make a list of all the toy stores and toy departments of larger stores that you think you could comfortably service in your area. It's then only a matter of visiting each one and explaining your service to the manager or the owner. Explain your business in terms of benefits to your prospect. If the owner spends time assembling toys, he's losing time that he could spend selling. If he doesn't bother to assemble the toys, tell him how many more sales he could possibly make if he sold the toys fully assembled to non-mechanically minded parents.

How to Promote.   You really can't advertise this service in the usual sense. The best way to sell it is by personal contact with likely prospects in your area.

Your Opportunity for Growth.   Once you get a reputation with toy dealers for careful work, it's only a small step to start handling all their repair work. And once this work is flowing, you can give some serious thought to opening your own fix-it shop—for both your present customers and for the parents themselves.

The skills used in this business lead themselves to other money-making opportunities. For example, you might consider custom lamp making, clock repair and even home repair consultant.

TRAILER AND CAMPER MAINTENANCE AND REPAIR

Hitch On to This Money-Maker

Your Opportunity for Profit.   The fastest growing recreational activity today is family camping, and campers and trailers have to be serviced and maintained. Unlike a car, which can be serviced by a local gas station, a camper has a lot of other things that demand the attention of a specialist. Many camper owners prefer not to do the work themselves and would just as soon let you take over the task. You'll make a nice profit, considering the hours you'll work.

This is a great job for a handyman who enjoys solving a million and one little problems—a folding table that doesn't fold . . . a pesky leak around a window . . . drawers that stick and doors that don't. Dozens of problems like this arise in every camper and only your thoughtful maintenance can solve them.

What You Can Earn. You'll be charging for parts and labor on your jobs. The exact charges will vary, but your time would bring at least $5 to $10 an hour.

You'll learn the similarities of the various types of campers and trailers after you've worked on a few. This simplifies your work once you get an idea of the more common problems you'll face. You should think of adopting a standard "ready" charge to inspect, adjust and make minor repairs to a standard camper.

Owners also have special needs and many times they will ask if you can customize some special detail or add something not originally installed as standard equipment—like a fold-down table, for example—and for these you'll have to develop a sense of estimating your time requirements.

HOW TO BUILD YOUR WEALTH BASE

Here's What You Need. You need an interest in working with tools. The work requires no more skill than is needed to do the hundred-and-one odd jobs around your own house or apartment —except that you'll be working in much more cramped quarters. Ordinary tools that you probably already own will do nicely. No equipment of a specialized nature is really needed.

How to Get Started. Begin by making yourself familiar with the different types of trailers and campers available. The easiest way to do this is to spend some time with various magazines that deal with camping and recreation.

While you are reading the magazines, answer the ads and so build a file of literature and specification on the various models, both ready-built and the ones sold in kit form. Write to the manu-facturers and ask them for service manuals. Even if you have to pay a few dollars for these, it will be worth it in time saved on the job.

How to Promote.   Unlike cars which can be serviced and re-paired at any gas station, camper repair and maintenance is usu-ally available only at the original dealer's place of business. This means that simple advertising in papers that cover the area you want to service will do a good job of generating business . . . Campers get to know each other and will carry recommendations of good service far and wide. Word-of-mouth advertising like this is impossible to beat—expecially considering that it is free.

Seek out the manager of the local sporting goods store or the camping department of a department store. Usually, you can work out a deal whereby you can display your sign, or a small counter display with your message and business cards.

Finally, if you're lucky enough to live near a main highway that carries a lot of campers to some camp ground or state park, see if you can get a sign or billboard to advertise your service.

Your Opportunity for Growth.   You can take on more and more work up to your seasonal limit. Then you should consider adding some full-time help. A college boy, or even a high-school senior who has a driver's license will be a great help. Install a trailer hitch on your own car, and you can offer a pick-up and delivery service with such a helper.

You can be the best judge of the potential of this business after you've worked at it for a while and seen it grow. More than likely, you will have enough saved from your earnings to consider open-ing a full-time camper sales showroom.

TRANSLATING AND INTERPRETING

From Fluency to Affluency

Your Opportunity for Profit.   George Thompson had a way with words. In fact, it was actually a hobby with him. Even though he never studied foreign languages formally, he had learned to speak both French and Italian as a child from his bilingual parents. When he was in service, this ability got him a good spot interpreting reports in these languages, and a feel for what he wanted to do when he left the service.

Today, George, and his wife live in a delightful seaside town, where he pursues his translating activities—by mail—far from the congestion of the city. Assignments are all handled by mail.

What You Can Earn.   Depending on the language, and the nature of the material to be translated, rates vary from less than a dollar per typewritten page to several dollars a page. Technical translation requires specific experience, plus the language skills, and is therefore worth more. Straight text translation of articles, and other easily translatable material, form the bulk of translation work. Depending on your fluency and the complexity of the material, you can earn up to $10 an hour for your work. George's annual income is seldom less than $18,000, and he has plenty of time to visit the nearby beach.

HOW TO BUILD YOUR WEALTH BASE

Here's What You Need.   You will, of course, need to be fluent in a foreign language. The only piece of equipment needed is a good typewriter. There are typewriter models which let you change keys for foreign language typing. Any typewriter store can give you the details.

How to Get Started.   Contact the larger universities, and the companies near you with international operations. These people often need help with the translation of foreign language journals. Publishers are also a good bet.

How to Promote.   Write letters to the sources mentioned, and keep in touch, either by phone, or with an occasional visit. You might run classified ads in the literary journals, and magazines aimed at the publishing field. The Freelancers Newsletter published by Jarrow Press, Inc., 1556 Third Ave., New York, N.Y. 10028 is also a good spot to put an ad. Write to them for rates.

Your Opportunity for Growth.   You can only do so much each day, no matter how much work you are offered. You might seek out people who speak other languages, so you can offer a broader and more complete service as a translating bureau.

TRUCK WASHING SERVICE

Haul in Clean Profits

Your Opportunity for Profit. Most small companies with a few trucks are often hard-pressed to keep them clean. The drivers' time is usually spread thin, and the trucks only see water when it rains. There are, in the larger metropolitan areas, automated truck washes, similar to the usual car wash, but they really are few and far between.

Clean trucks create a favorable image wherever they travel. If you couple this statement with the fact that you can wash the trucks without creating costly "downtime," you'll have an attractive offer for every owner of a truck fleet.

What You Can Earn. Use the pointers we discussed in the first chapter to figure hourly charges. Because a larger truck takes more time, you will, obviously, charge more for a large truck. Don't quote an hourly charge to your customer, but use your rate to estimate a price. For example: if you feel it will take an hour to wash a certain truck, and you have set your hourly rate at $6 per hour, you should charge $6 plus the cost of the supplies you use up.

If you are competing with an automated truck wash, it is not always necessary to beat them on price. Simply tell the owner that you do the work when the truck is not working—evenings or weekends—saving him a loss of delivery time.

HOW TO BUILD YOUR WEALTH BASE

Here's What You Need. Tools required for this service are simple and inexpensive. A large hose-swab is all-important. This is a mop-like arrangement at the end of a long pipe, which is connected to a hose. They usually have attachments for applying liquid soap as the water flows. At least 50 feet of lightweight plastic hose, a pail, rags and several sponges complete the basic kit. A supply of several types of wax should be stocked for when a wax job is needed. Of course, you'll need transportation to get to-and-from your customers' sites. Your own car is more than adequate.

How to Get Started.   Make a list of all the companies within a few miles of your home with their own trucks. Try to select those with more than one. It seldom pays to make a trip to clean one truck. Look in the yellow pages for such companies as delivery services, furniture stores, department stores, major appliance stores, and other businesses which must deliver their products.

How to Promote.   You can either make up a small mailer and send it to them, or make a personal visit to the company traffic manager. A combination of the two, mailing first, then calling a week or so later is always the best. Be sure to point out the image a clean truck produces in the mind of their customers.

Contact the local chamber of commerce and advertise in their newsletter. If there are any local trade associations, be sure to run an ad in their magazines. Get in touch with the truck dealers and have them give you a recommendation.

Your Opportunity for Growth.   You can only wash so many trucks in a day. Hire a crew when the business gets going. The best source of workers are high-school students looking for part-time dollars. If you do use them, be sure to check up on the laws governing the employment of minors. Working papers are required in some states for certain types of jobs.

UNDERGROUND SPRINKLER
SYSTEM INSTALLATION

Make the Money Flow for You

Your Opportunity for Profit.   Nobody has to tell you that taking care of the lawn is the great American weekend chore. Those who can afford the service, will hire a lawn maintenance firm to do the cutting, fertilizing, and weeding. But one job remains for the homeowner—watering the lawn. No amount of care will take the place of thorough, regular watering. And the best way to water a lawn is by means of a built-in sprinkler system.

Too few homeowners think of a sprinkler system for their lawns because they are unaware that it is relatively easy and inexpensive to install. Old-fashioned systems required regular metal pipe and experienced plumbing know-how for installation. With the new plastic pipe available, you can do a good job of installing an underground sprinkler system with nothing more complicated than a straight shovel and a hacksaw. The water connection is made by an ordinary hose coupling to the outside water faucet so there is no fussy plumbing work to do.

Install a system in your own lawn. That will give you all the experience you need to go out and do the job for others and add to your Wealth Base. This is a great extra service to offer in combination with the several other outdoor maintenance businesses we've described in this book—lawn maintenance, landscape planning, driveway sealing, and the like.

What You Can Earn.   After you've installed your own system, you'll have a good idea of the amount of time the installation of a system will require, and also enable you to estimate the amount of materials you'll need to cover a given area of ground.

To estimate a job, add the cost of your materials, (which you can buy wholesale once you've established yourself as a professional), and the hours you'll need to do the job. Chapter 1 told you how to figure your hourly rate, so adding up the cost of the job is relatively easy. It shouldn't be hard to pocket $75 to $100 for a day's work. The materials will come to perhaps a third of the amount, so you will still have a neat profit to tally.

HOW TO BUILD YOUR WEALTH BASE

Here's What You Need.   The plastic pipe is sold by major mail order houses, garden supply shops, and hardware stores. Most of them have instructions available for the installation of the pipe. Basically, the plastic pipe is cut with a fine saw. Joints are made with plastic couplings and special plastic cement. There is no threading or complicated cutting. The trench that the pipe is buried in is simply a deep slit in the ground that you made with a long, straight spade.

How to Get Started.   Again, this is a great business to build via the "neighborhood cruise" that we suggested in other places in the book. Look for homes with fussy lawns—you can be sure the owner is spending a lot of money to keep it up and will probably be a good prospect for an underground sprinkler system.

New people moving into the neighborhood are usually good prospects, because many times they have great ideas on decorating and landscaping their new home and readily agree to the installation of a system.

How to Promote.   The simplest promotion is to call on likely prospects you uncover in your travels. Or, you can note the addresses of likely prospects and send them a letter with an estimate already attached. Follow up with a phone call a few days later.

Include a mention of this service in any other advertising you may do to promote the other businesses you may be running. Generally speaking, this advertising will be limited to the classified pages of your local newspaper and your telephone directory.

Your Opportunity for Growth.   This is a great "plus" to add to your other businesses. Your growth will come as these other businesses prosper. Once installed, there is virtually no maintenance needed on the system, so you quickly run out of prospects. But, even a small town can easily provide you with a hundred or so customers in a short period of time, the income from which can come to a mighty impressive total.

Be sure to contact the offices in your area with lawns. This "commercial" work can be a good source of business.

UPHOLSTERY

Building a Profitable Future for You

Your Opportunity for Profit. It's hard to think of anyone who doesn't have at least one upholstered item in his home. And, if it's being used, it's being worn out—and thus provides another opportunity for the person aware of the profits to be made in the custom upholstery business.

Many otherwise knowledgeable people shy away from this field of activity because they think it requires a great investment in materials, or requires years of arduous experience to qualify as a skilled worker in the field. Nothing could be further from the truth.

What You Can Earn. Let's say the diner down the street has 10 booths with a pair of upholstered seats or benches. Re-doing just one booth is easily worth $150 in today's market. The materials will probably cost you $25, leaving you a profit of $125—and this for only about 8 hours work! In two weeks, you could do all 10 booths and be $1250 richer. Do it on your vacation, or after hours, or on weekends. Anyway you add it up, there is a good profit to be made in this business.

HOW TO BUILD YOUR WEALTH BASE

Here's What You Need. You will need some basic training in custom upholstery. Fortunately, there are a number of schools offering courses. If you want to study by mail, you can check with the Modern Upholstery Institute, P. O. Box 899, Orange, California 92669.

Equally important, the tools you need for this business are few and very inexpensive. A few hammers, webbing stretchers, scissors, and tape, and you're in business. Your biggest investment will be in supplies, which you can buy as you need them in relatively small quantities.

How to Get Started. You probably have some pieces of your

own on which you can practice. By the time they're finished, you should have enough confidence to go out and do expensive custom jobs for pay.

You can do work for both businesses and for private individuals. In the first case, you should list all your potential customers —restaurants, hotels, motels, and business offices. As for individuals, just about everyone is a prospect.

How to Promote.   Call in person on your larger business prospects, and suggest how modernization and re-upholstery will improve the appearance of their premises or offices and attract new business for them.

Private trade can be gotten with regular advertising in the local newspaper and in the telephone directory. Certain people are more likely to be prospects than others. For example: people who have just moved into a new house, or have had their home redecorated will many times be moved to reupholster their furniture since it looks shabby in new surroundings.

Your Opportunity for Growth.   This is the kind of business that quickly grows by referrals and word of mouth advertising as you gain a reputation among the people you do work for. Also, when you do one piece for a customer, you can always suggest that another piece should also be done.

USED TOOL EXCHANGE

Build a Fortune with Other People's Tools

Your Opportunity for Profit.   Bill Harrison bought a modest home in the suburbs, and soon found a number of projects that demanded the use of power tools. Like thousands of homeowners before him, Bill bought some power tools, made some of the projects he promised himself he would do, and then lost all interest in woodworking as a hobby.

When a friend asked him about the dust-covered power saw in his basement, Bill jokingly offered to sell it to him at about half the original cost. His friend snapped it up, and gave Bill the idea of buying and selling unwanted tools. In fact, he later bought back his original saw, and re-sold it at a profit. Of course, he soon outgrew his garage, and ran out of spare time to keep up with the activity. Today, Bill runs the business full-time, and makes money from sales of new and used tools, as well as tool rentals.

What You Can Earn.   Many people, when they lose interest in power tools will almost give them away to get them out from under foot. This price is often as low as one-third of the new price. For example, a radial saw that sold for about $250, will often be disposed of for less than half its cost. You can take this $100 bargain—clean, adjust, and sharpen it—and sell it for a 50% mark-up or $150.

If, while the saw is resting in your display space, someone wants to rent it, you can make even more money. To figure the rental rate, find out what the commercial rentals are charging and reduce the rate by 10%. You then have a legitimate reason for offering the "discount." You are renting used equipment. Few people will stop to realize that the other rentals are also renting "used" gear.

In an area packed with do-it-yourself addicts, this business can net you in excess of $20,000 for a full time operation.

HOW TO BUILD YOUR WEALTH BASE

Here's What You Need.   Space! Start in your garage, but when it turns full-time, you must rent a store with plenty of space. Don't head for the high-rent district. When people look for used bargains, they don't expect to find them in the posh down-town locations. You'll save on rent, too.

How to Get Started.   If you don't have any friends with tools to sell, run a few ads in the classified pages. Most papers have a used tool heading that you can use. You can also consider operating as a consignment shop initially to conserve capital. Doing this, you will earn less, but you can avoid the risk of losing your capital.

How to Promote.   To sell the tools you now have, simply run ads in the same columns, and send out regular post-card mailers to new homeowners in your area. Post notices in cooperating lumberyards, and be sure to spread the word with your friends and business associates. In addition, a sure-fire promotion technique is to display some of your smaller tools at garage sales run by others. Arrange with the homeowner running the sale, or the garage sale consultant (described elsewhere in this book) for the display, and split the profits.

Your Opportunity for Growth.   Besides simply increasing your volume by buying and selling more tools, you might consider adding the medical equipment exchange we have described elsewhere in this book. It's a natural addition, because the methods of doing business are very much alike.

VISUAL AIDS PRODUCTION

How to Show Profits for Yourself

Your Opportunity for Profit.   "Visual instructional media" is a forbiddingly high-sounding name. But that is what professional teachers call anything you look at that teaches or tells you something. And, it's more than just a fancy name for a chart to tack on the board. Visual instructional media covers all sorts of illustrations done in every conceivable manner, photographs, drawings, transparencies, slides, and anything else that can be used for teaching by sight.

Curiously enough, professional teachers know what to say on a chart or a transparency, but are usually unskilled in the "how" techniques of producing charts. You can capitalize on this by studying some of the more common techniques and then selling

this new found talent of yours. You will find it remarkably easy.
What You Can Earn. Most of your clients will be teachers in industry—company training directors, sales managers, and the like. They have budgets to spend on professionally-prepared learning materials because they are so important in their work. You will be charging for your time plus the cost of any materials you may use. At $10 an hour, you can easily net $100 to $150 for a weekend's work.

HOW TO BUILD YOUR WEALTH BASE

Here's What You Need. Art talent is definitely not needed. Most of the work is done with the materials and devices that take the place of skill. There are lettering machines and stencils, paper "type" that is pasted down, embossing and laminating presses to print and protect, and dozens of other items.

If this area is somewhat new to you, then a trip to the library is in order. One of the best books we can recommend is *Techniques for Producing Visual Instructional Media* by Ed Minor and Harvey R. Frye, and published by McGraw-Hill, New York, N.Y. 10036.
How to Get Started. Get some books and study the simpler techniques. Then get some materials and practice. The best thing you can practice on is your "presentation" book. This is usually a large loose-leaf book in which you can put samples of your work, and then take around to potential clients.
How to Promote. Call on the training directors and other purchasers of educational materials at local companies. Many times, you will discover that they are desperate for a source of charts, slides, and other devices they need for their teaching sessions. Often they will be getting them done in a very amateurish way by a clerk in the department, or they will be spending too much money on the project having an expensive engineering draftsman take time out to letter some charts. You can solve both these problems at a savings to the company and with profit to yourself.
Your Opportunity for Growth. Your growth is dependent on how much time you want to invest in this business and the potential you have for sales in your area. You can, with some investment in promotion, try to develop additional business by mail.

With several good clients, you can soon consider turning to this business as a source of full-time income.

WANT-AD PRESS PUBLISHING

Advertise for Dollars

Your Opportunity for Profit.   How would you like to make a handsome profit on everything you sell—be able to sell just about everything—and never handle the product, or even see the person who buys it? Sounds like a pipe-dream, doesn't it? Well, it isn't, and all it takes is a little effort, less than $100, and some determination. The business with all these features is the "want-ad press."

Everybody has something to sell. Here's your chance to make money on this very real situation. You publish a simple flyer, listing everybody's valuable "junk." Nobody pays you a cent until they sell something. Then you collect your commission.

What You Can Earn.   Set up a fixed schedule of commissions immediately. It should be based on major classes of products. Here's the schedule for one of the more successful classified ad papers. Use it only for a comparative guide, and adjust the commissions according to what you feel your particular area can support:

- general merchandise—10%
- cars, motorcycles, etc.—5%
- houses—2%
- lots and acreage—4%
- rooms for rent—20% of first month's rent
- business opportunities—4%

You can begin by giving your publication away at no cost. After it catches on, charge a quarter a copy if you have 10 or fewer pages—50¢ for more than 10 pages. These flyers seldom exceed 30 pages an issue, and can make the publisher in excess of $30,000 a year.

HOW TO BUILD YOUR WEALTH BASE

Here's What You Need.   To begin with, you must have some method of duplicating a few hundred copies of your ad sheet. Check with several local printers for competitive prices. Don't waste time and money with fancy art-work. It really should not look too good. After all, you are selling second-hand merchandise and the people reading your sheet are looking for bargains. A slick job might even frighten people away. You'll also need someone who can type. The printer will often do this for less than $2 a page.

How to Get Started.   Start by asking your twenty nearest neighbors to give you a list of things they would like to sell. Be sure to tell them that they do not pay you a cent until the item has been sold. Then they only owe you a commission, based on the rates you established. Collections are seldom a problem, even though you are working on the honor system. When you have enough items to fill four or five typewritten pages, begin to classify them according to general product types. For the best system, check the titles used by your local newspaper for their own classified pages.

How to Promote.   The publication is its own best promotion. You might consider offering special rates to charitable organizations for their sales, if their members will buy a number of copies. A good bet is to get the kids to peddle it door-to-door.

Have the local candy store take a stack. You can let him keep half the proceeds of selling the little paper.

Your Opportunity for Growth.   Obviously, this business has the seeds of its own growth built right in. Everybody has a closet full of junk they would like to get rid of—and there is always someone who is just as interested in filling up his closet with someone else's junk. You simply provide the medium, and collect money for the service. You expand by getting more advertisers and more stores to carry the copies.

WINDOW DECORATING

Get Paid for Showing Off Your Talents

Your Opportunity for Profit.   If you're one of those persons who thoroughly enjoys window shopping—particularly if you find yourself drawn to attractive displays in store windows—then you might just have an undiscovered talent that can earn you money as a window decorator.

Robert Levin ran a busy stationery store, and always tried to handle his windows himself. He crammed it full of just everything, thinking that this was the way to sell. The result was a hopeless jumble—so much to see that no one really saw anything at all!

When one of the store employees found enough nerve to tell him so, the owner took his advice and hired a professional window trimmer to do the job. Even if it cost him $100 for one day of the man's time, he quickly paid for it out of increased interest in his store and greater traffic through his door. So pleased was he with the results that eventually the window trimmer came back on a regular basis to handle the windows.

What You Can Earn.   Depending on your experience, you can earn $50 to $100 a day for your work. But, even with little more than your own good taste, you can expect to earn $25 to $50 for decorating the windows of an average store. You will be selling your ideas to the store owner, and it will be your ideas that will count, rather than the number of hours you spend arranging merchandise in the window.

HOW TO BUILD YOUR WEALTH BASE

Here's What You Need.   Take a walk down the main street of your town with your eyes open. If you find yourself mentally rating the various window displays you see, then you probably have the sense of design and good taste essential to success.

While you're out, stop off at the library and see what books or other publications might be available for study. Decorating a window follows much the same principles that are important in decorating a home—color selection, harmony, balance, center of interest, and so on. If there are no books on window decorating as such, you can still pick up scores of ideas from the many books on interior decorating and design.

The basic tools you'll need are few and inexpensive—tackhammer, stapler, pliers, scissors, and tacks. Take along a pair of soft-soled bedroom slippers that you can wear in the window, and, if you happen to be a woman, a pair of slacks.

How to Get Started. Find a small store or shop that seems to cry for help. Be honest, and tell the owner you are just starting out, and that you'll do his window without charge. Free offers like this can make people suspicious of some "catch". The "catch" is simply this: when finished, you want his permission to photograph the window and use it to show off your talents to other prospects.

How to Promote. Get extra copies of the photo you've made of the window. Take them to other stores in the neighborhood, and invite them to inspect your work on display nearby. Few merchants will decide on the spot. Therefore, you should leave some sort of card or reminder that will let them get in touch with you when they get around to changing their windows. Be persistent and don't be afraid to keep following up at intervals of every few weeks.

Be a "joiner" and support your local merchants' associations. Offer your services to the local Chamber of Commerce as a speaker, and take advantage of every opportunity to get involved with their problems. At intervals, send reminders to the merchants and suggest seasonal windows.

Your Opportunity for Growth. Once your reputation has been established, you'll have to think of adding assistants to your staff. When they reach a satisfactory level of performance, you won't even have to check the windows they do. You can prepare a basic sketch for your helper and let it go at that.

At this point, most of your work will be in building your business, designing windows, and handling the administrative details of your business. Your bedroom slippers will have been retired for some time.

This is an ideal business to create additional opportunities in sign making and even the visual aids production that are described elsewhere in the book.

WRITING SHORT PARAGRAPHS

Pen Your Way to Profit

Your Opportunity for Profit.   Have you ever wondered just who writes those short paragraphs in the hobby, handyman, and home magazines? You know, the 50-word "fillers" that give such hints as how to store nails in baby food jars, and how women can shorten their hours in the kitchen. Well, they are written by the country's highest paid writers. They are people with a specific interest, hobby, or talent, but with usually *no formal training* in the craft of writing. They are able to write a few simple paragraphs about their hobby that will be of interest to others, and they make more money per word than many of the best-selling novelists.

John Steele, working his way through college in Ohio, supplemented his modest means by writing such material for the photo magazines. He was an amateur photographer, and simply sent along his ideas to the editors. The checks rolled back, in return. Today, he's a top publishing executive, but he still finds time to send in filler material whenever he comes up with an idea in his hobby darkroom.

What You Can Earn.   We mentioned that most of these people are untrained, yet are the highest paid writers in the business. It's true. When you consider that some editors will pay $50 or more for as few as 50 words, you get the picture. And when editors start contacting you with specific assignments, you will really hit the big money. John wasn't looking to make a lot of money—only school expenses. This he did, and found that with a little extra effort he could have made over $7,000 a year.

HOW TO BUILD YOUR WEALTH BASE

Here's What You Need. Believe it or not, you don't even need a typewriter, although it does help. All it takes are ideas. Editors buy ideas that will interest readers. They don't care if it's typed on special paper, or written on notepaper, as long as it is legible and has editorial merit. But, just being a householder looking for the easiest way to get a job done, is often all it takes to get these money-making ideas.

How to Get Started. How did you simplify that last gutter installation? No one was around to hold it in place while you set the nails. You used an old coat hanger, hooked around the roofing nails, under the shingles as a sling—and it worked. Of course! Now write about it.

When you begin the actual writing, pick up several copies of the major magazines that cover your field of interest. Look for the "filler" material and read every one closely. Study the style. Note that this is short, terse, and very direct writing. This is the style you must master. Actually, it's quite easy because it is almost the same as you would speak, if you were talking to someone about the project. In fact, this is a good way to get the feel for this kind of writing.

There are a number of courses offered by correspondence on this subject. If you would like a simple manual that gives you a self-coaching "check list" and an up-to-date list of editors who buy from beginners. Send for details to James Franklin Associates, Box 95, Demarest, New Jersey 07627.

How to Promote. You simply do not promote this work. What you do is send your material directly to an editor, along with a simple cover letter. Be sure to include a stamped, self-addressed envelope for returns. If the editor likes your work, you will get a check in return. If he doesn't, you will get your copy back.

When your copy comes back, don't be discouraged. Simply put

it in another envelope and send it to the next editor on your list. The Franklin Letter checklist mentioned above contains the actual names and addresses of the filler-buying editors, and it is updated regularly for the convenience of filler writers, such as yourself.

Your Opportunity for Growth.   Nothing succeeds like success, and this field is one of the best examples of this adage. As the editors come to recognize your contributions, they will seek you out with special assignments. And, too, you will probably want to try your hand at some other kinds of writing. Short stories, children's stories, feature-length hobby articles—they all represent high-pay outlets for the writer who wants to write for money and to see his name in print.

With your writing skills polished from this experience, you might consider taking a crack at the "good buy" press business we have described. If you have the duplicating equipment for this business, "jobbing" other printing is a natural.

YARD MAINTENANCE

Keep Your Wallet Green

Your Opportunity for Profit.   Most homeowners turn lawn and garden care into a back-breaking job because they try to do too many jobs by using hand tools. Hand tools have their place in garden care, but a self-propelled mower, for example, can do a lot more work than a mower you have to push. Unfortunately, many of the machines that can make quick work of garden tasks seem like an extravagance for the average owner. Here's where you can profit two ways:

1. You can make money taking care of people's yards
2. You can take care of your own yard with machines that you formerly thought would be too expensive for you to acquire

What it boils down to is simply this: you get all the power tools and machines you dream about, and then pay off the investment in a season or two by doing jobs for other people.

What You Can Earn. It's surprising how few people think of this way to make money. Greg Swanson, just turned 16, saw the opportunity not so long ago. He had saved up $400 from his paper routes during the previous years. His father loaned him another $200, and with this $600, Greg invested in a large riding-type mower. He was smart enough to add some accessories—a dozer blade for snow removal during the winter months, and other items for mulching and picking up debris.

Greg bought the mower at a sale near the end of the summer. Before next spring rolled around, Greg had paid off his whole investment just clearing snow from driveways for his neighbors. The money he made later that summer was pure profit. You can take a lesson from a young boy and do just as well.

HOW TO BUILD YOUR WEALTH BASE

Here's What You Need. You may already have an efficient machine that can earn money for you. Few people really capitalize on the investments they already made. So look around your garage and take stock of the jobs you can do for hire with the stuff you already own.

Going beyond what you now own will be up to you. Mowers, mulchers, thatchers, and a host of other tools and machines can make short work of many irksome jobs.

How to Get Started. Decide on the machine that will give you the most capabilities. Greg's choice of a riding mower with accessories is a good point to keep in mind. Learn to use the machine if it is new to you when it is delivered. You have to get some proficiency in turning tight corners, avoiding bushes, and the like.

How to Promote. Just riding around in your own yard will be great promotion. Once you tell your neighbors that you're in business, you'll be surprised how quick the calls will come in. Another good way to get your name in front of a lot of people is to offer to mow the lawn or clear the driveways of a local church, lodge, or similar organization for free, or for a very nominal sum. Your name will come up often in meetings of that group!

Your Opportunity for Growth.   Yard care can become a full time business if you want to go beyond the neighborhood. Ideally, you can add this service to any of the several outdoor businesses we have been showing you in the pages of this book.

3

You Have to Tell to Sell

Someone one said, "Nothing happens until someone makes a sale." What he meant is simply this: all the great enterprises of the world are built on sales. No business can grow and prosper unless there is someone out there selling. Yet, the fear of selling is probably the number one reason why most otherwise capable people never start a business, or why most businesses that are started quickly fail.

Too many people dread the thought of selling. What do you say? What do you do when the prospect says "No" flatly to your face? How do you find the courage to go on? These are the kind of needless fears that go round and round in people's minds.

Selling Can Be the Most Exciting Thing You Do. At the beginning of this book we gave you a business secret. "Find a human need, satisfy it, and you will become rich." Now we will give you a selling secret. Once you learn to apply it you will look upon selling, not as something to be feared, but as one of the most rewarding and satisfying things you can do in life. Moreover, as you discover this secret in your life, you will start selling yourself and your business in so many subtle ways that personal success and wealth will be drawn to you almost by magic.

Again, we can best describe this secret by means of an example. Here are two salesmen and their opening remarks to a prospect.

"Would you be interested in buying some more insurance?" says one.

"I want to share some good news with you," says the other. "Now you can be sure that Jane and Billy will be able to attend that college you have in mind for them . . . my company just found a way to guarantee it for a person like yourself."

Even if you've never sold anything in your life, you know that the second salesman will stand a better chance of getting the prospect to put his name on the dotted line, and *even thank the salesman for the opportunity.* Let's see why. If we do, the selling secret will become known to us.

What Is Selling?   Look up the word "sell" in any dictionary and you will see why it strikes dread in the hearts of the inexperienced. A typical definition runs like this: *"to sell"*—"to transfer ownership of something for payment of one kind or another." What the dictionary is defining is the legal *act* of selling, the formal "closing" of a deal.

Right here is the problem. Most often, people who know nothing about selling confuse the legal act of selling with what you do to attract people to your offer. The wise salesman knows that the legal act of selling, or the "close," comes only *after* the application of a number of simple selling principles that automatically lead the prospect to say "yes" at the close of a deal.

Forget the dictionary definition right now. Instead, memorize this definition of "selling" which is our favorite:

"To sell is to want something good for another person, and to go out of your way to make sure it happens."

This statement contains the secret of selling. If you discover a need in a person's life and then show how your product or service will benefit that need, then you are engaged in selling as we define the word. The key word here is "benefit."

Show a person the benefits that can be his and his natural self-interest will do the rest. Our hypothetical prospect in the beginning of this chapter is not interested in merely buying insurance.

But, he is interested in providing for his children's education. That's why you can be sure the second salesman will get the nod. He could spot the need, and then made his offer in terms of benefits to his prospect.

How to Apply This Selling Secret.   Once you have grasped the full meaning of the word "sell" then you can apply it in every aspect of your business. Every statement you make, whether it's in person at the front door of a prospect, in an ad that appears in the paper, or in a letter that you mailed to potential customers, it should always be built on the foundation of *benefits*.

Whenever you address a prospect, think of our definition of selling—to want something good to happen to a person, and to go out of your way to make sure it happens. Selling then becomes both enjoyable and exciting. Instead of looking for a rebuff, you can be sure that a prospect will instantly react to your offer with interest. You're not at his door to relieve him of a sum of money. You're there because you have something of benefit to him. And, when you phrase your offer in terms of benefits, you have no trouble with a prospect listening to you.

Throughout this book we have mentioned ways of promoting certain businesses. Now we will show you how to apply this selling secret to the more common promotion methods you'll be engaged in with your spare-time business.

Direct Selling.   This is the simplest and the oldest selling method. It is a face-to-face situation where you outline the benefits of your product or service to a prospect. Even if you've aroused the interest of a prospect by means of an ad or a mailing, the final part of the sale usually is done in person. Here are some pointers to keep in mind:

1. *Think benefits!* Above everything else, all your statements must be in terms of benefits to the prospect. You are there because you can help satisfy some need. With this thought foremost in your mind, you will eliminate 99% of your fears of dealing with strangers.
2. *Know your product or service!* This means doing a fair amount of homework before you start selling. The purpose behind this study is to make sure you can answer any question a customer can bring up. Nothing inspires confidence as much as a salesperson who really knows what he is talking about.

3. *Make a presentation!* Don't be content to let the prospect ask questions and then answer them. *You* have to control the interview, and you do it very simply. Have a story to tell about your business. Outline the benefits, show how you can help the prospect enjoy these benefits, and suggest why he should decide now. If you have this presentation outlined in a brochure that you can leave with the prospect, so much the better.

How to Make Advertising Work for You. If you've listened carefully to what we've said about selling, then you're capable right now to turn out a professional advertisement. Forgetting for a moment all the types of advertising available to you, they all have one thing in common:

Advertising is simply communicating your message of benefits to as many people as possible.

It's that simple! But you should know some of the types of advertising most effective for the small businessman.

NEWSPAPERS

Your local paper is probably one of the best sources of business, and you should visit the business department of your paper early in your business career.

The advertising manager of the paper will be glad to give you a "rate card." This is a printed information card that gives information on costs, closing dates, special charges, and anything else you might want to know about the paper before you invest money in an ad. Space in the newspaper is sold by the "line" or the "column inch." These charges usually refer to what is known as "display" space in the regular pages of the newspaper.

Space in the classified section of a paper is usually sold by the word or the line. Every classified section has headings that sort out the ads into special classifications—"articles for sale," "dance instruction," "personals," and so on. If yours is the only business of its kind that is appearing in the classified section, you can sometimes get the paper to run it under its own special heading at no extra cost. Take advantage of this fact.

Another hint to keep in mind: almost all space in newspapers is available on a "contract rate." This means you agree to take a certain amount of space during a period of time. In return for this, the newspaper will give you a discount on the advertising charges, depending on how much space you contract for, and how frequently you plan on running your ads.

Don't be afraid of the word "contract." There's nothing in the contract to force you take the amount of advertising you agreed to take. If you take less space than the contract calls for, you are merely billed at the rate that would be in effect if you didn't have a contract, and you are *billed only for the space you actually use.* A lot of businessmen shy away from a contract arrangement and wind up spending more money on advertising than they would if they had simply asked for a contract rate in the beginning.

OTHER PRINT ADVERTISING

Advertising in magazines is not usually very practical for the small or local businessman. Magazines generally have a circulation in locations far beyond what you could reasonably service. The one exception to this statement is the mail-order business. If you are selling anything by mail, then you want as much circulation all over the country as you can possibly get.

Magazine space is sold very much like space in newspapers, and contract rates are also available. As a rule, we would suggest you avoid spending money in souvenir programs, and other "one-shot" publications. Advertising, to be effective, must be repeated, which is impossible in publications of this type.

MAIL ADVERTISING

The first thing you should do after you decide to go into business is to visit your postmaster. Every smart businessman gets Uncle Sam to work for him as a partner. There are a number of ways you can build business via the mails:

1. *Ordinary postcards.* You can type and mail them to prospects as we have suggested in many places in the previous pages. If you want to mail more than a hundred, then get a

printer to print the message for you. Small mimeographs are available that are designed just for printing postcards and are handy gadgets. If you spoil any cards, return them to the postoffice for a refund of the postage.

2. *Letters.* Again, these can be individually prepared letters or printed and mailed in fair quantities. If you plan on mailing any quantity at all, check your postmaster for information on a bulk mailing permit. This permits you to mail letters at lower, third-class mail rates.

3. *Reply envelopes.* If you want your prospect to mail something back to you, make sure you provide a business-reply envelope. Again, you get a permit at the postoffice, which then lets you print business reply envelopes. Your customer pays no postage on these, and you pay postage only on those that are actually mailed back to you.

4. *Other services.* Tell your postmaster what you have in mind. He will be able to suggest other services available through the post office that will help you build your business—mail forwarding, information on new addresses, and the like.

TELEPHONE DIRECTORY ADVERTISING

This can be a most effective form of advertising for certain types of services. Generally speaking, the service should be the sort that is not habitually used by a customer. For example: a person goes to a grocery store very frequently; it would be rather wasteful for a grocer to advertise here, because people don't normally have to hunt for a grocer.

On the other hand, if you restore antiques, an ad in the yellow pages would be quite natural. People normally don't have antiques restored every day. When they do need such a service, the first place they usually think to look is in the directory. Keep this principle in mind if you plan directory advertising.

Directory advertising is sold on an annual basis, but you have the opportunity to pay for the service monthly with your phone bill. The unfortunate thing is that you cannot start or stop directory advertising as easily as you can advertising in newspapers.

OTHER FORMS OF ADVERTISING

Once you've been in business for a time, you will be solicited for just about every type of advertising imaginable. Radio and TV spots, imprinted specialty items, matchbooks, and a host of other offers will be made to you. There is no simple rule to help you decide which type of advertising would be useful. It all depends on the individual case.

The best advice we can give is this: refer back to the pages describing your business, or a business similar to the one you're operating. In the various sections on "How to Promote" we've given you advice on what types of advertising would be most effective for a particular business and the reasons why. Use these statements as a guide.

Another rule to remember is this: don't buy advertising because it is a "bargain," or because it simply reaches a lot of people. Ask a lot of questions before you spend money on any type of advertising. The question that must be answered to your satisfaction is this: how many *real prospects* does this ad reach, and how much is it costing me to reach each of these prospects?

A Final Word.   In the beginning, you will most probably depend a lot on direct selling of your services. This, combined with the natural word-of-mouth advertising that your business generates, can bring you all the work you can reasonably handle. Once you decide to advertise, make the decision and stick to it.

Set apart a certain amount of money that will be spent on advertising, and then *spend it,* even if the initial results are disappointing. The biggest mistake most beginners make in this field is to expect miracles from their very first ad.

4

Don't Re-Invent the Wheel

Profit by the Secret Discoveries of Others

There are literally thousands of ways to build an automatic, little or no investment Wealth Base. We have described 100 Wealth-Base businesses in detail that should appeal to just about every reader of this book. Some readers will start one and be immediately successful, while others, who might start the same business, may linger on the edge of success for a long period of time.
What causes such variation?

Luck?
Hardly.

Hard work?
Partially.

Inside information?
Yes . . . but it is information that is readily available to you if

you only know where to look. The secrets of business success have been learned by everyone who has built a business, but those who have been successful faster have either known these secrets, in advance, or have been quick to discover that it is not necessary for them to go thru the learning processes themselves.

Find Out What Sells Well.   Consider the case of William Carter, who wanted to start a mail-order business, but was not at all sure what he could sell successfully. Like many tyros in this field, he went the route of trying to invent a new gadget that would make him a million. Unfortunately, the Hula Hoop doesn't come along that often, and for every one that does succeed, hundreds of even better ideas fail. Fortunately, Bill didn't invest too much money and time in his projects, but one day while reading the classified ads in *Popular Mechanics*, he was struck by the similarity of some of the ads.

To confirm what appeared to be repeated ads, Bill got out some back issues of *Popular Mechanics* and similar magazines, and to his astonishment, found that the same ads appeared month-after-month, and in many of the magazines.

Until then, Bill had thought of these pages as only a place to sell or swap old equipment, but he had just made a discovery that was worth a fortune to him. There were companies who used these little classified ads to run large, national businesses.

Bill had learned, almost by accident, a "truth" that makes money every time for the mail-order man:

- *Don't re-invent the wheel.*

To find a money-making product, simply discover what other people are selling successfully, and either make it better, sell it for less, or do a better job of promotion, and you'll have it made.

Don't Be Afraid to Imitate.   This might rub you the wrong way, at first. "After all, it's new ideas that make fortunes, but the steady Wealth-Base Builders are made by automatically pyramiding capital from doing something that someone else has done to satisfy a need, but in some way, making it better.

When you have your Wealth Base well established, then you can afford to experiment with new ideas. At this point, you can afford to lose a few thousand dollars if an idea doesn't sell, but when you are first starting out, try something tried-and-true, but make sure that you do a better job in at least one of these ways:

- Sell your product or service at a better price
- Do a better job of advertising
- Produce a better product

You can profit by the discoveries of others, and often it's a lot safer than testing an entirely new idea.

Use Success Tested Methods. Most of the businesses in this book have tested business methods behind them. As professional marketing men, we have seen positive proof that many of these businesses have made fortunes for the people who have started them. We have seen people take ideas from one business and apply them to other businesses which have been of greater interest to them and build what have appeared on the surface to be entirely new businesses.

The businesses might appear to be new, but the success-factors borrowed from one business to boost another business into the black-ink were all tested and proven to be workable by others. You can do the same, regardless of the business you choose to start.

Many people are bothered by the idea of "lifting" an idea and applying it to their business. They often feel that their business should be totally the product of their imagination and efforts. This is truly a noble ambition, but just how many people have all the skills necessary to be such a one-man-band? There is nothing wrong with capitalizing on what has been successful for another in your own business. That is, unless you use private information to damage a competitor. And, then, there are laws that protect the businessman from such activity. But simply improving a product that someone else has sold successfully, only makes good business sense.

Extra Income Without Work. To further profit by the experience of others, you should re-focus your view on the world. As you ride to work each day, you get to learn the passing scene by heart. There's a gas station on that corner, and a grocery store on the next block. And so it goes until you reach your place of work. Try this little experiment tomorrow, on your way to work;

• As you ride to work you will notice that you have acquired particular habits—that is, at such-and-such a block you will always look to the left. Now—look to the right and make a conscious effort to see something *new* in every block. That is, something new to you. It may have been there all along, but you have just never paid any attention to it.

• You will find that it is as though you had never been this route before. After you have done this for a few days, decide that you are going to find a need to satisfy from this fresh view, and the business with which to do it. For example, suppose that you began to notice that many of the stores had no signs in the windows, and that the windows were poorly decorated. Here's a need, and, if you were so inclined, you could start a sign and window trimming business.

• After you have done this little exercise for several weeks, you will find yourself bursting with ways to make money by satisfying a need. In fact, you should keep a little notebook handy to jot the ideas down as they come to you.

Now that you have discovered all these crying needs, you profit by the experience of others by going about satisfying these needs with our success-tested methods. Take the sign and the window trimming example. We have shown in this book, how such businesses can be a very exciting Wealth-Base Builder. Many of the little hints we gave have resulted from the trials of others. We have, obviously, eliminated that which will not work, but have passed on, in detail, all of the success-laden tips that one could need in starting such a business.

In addition to this important way in insuring success, you should begin reading regularly as many publications as possible that would be relevant to your specific business, and business success in general.

One of the best sources of up-to-date information for the Wealth-Base Builder is *The Franklin Letter,* a confidential monthly service of James Franklin Associates. This copyrighted publication is sent to subscribers, and features a wealth of information and idea starters that both the beginning Wealth-Base Builder and the successful businessman can use to build wealth. For a one-year subscription, send $18 to James Franklin Associates, P. O. Box 95, Demarest, New Jersey 07627.

Other great sources of important information include the local office of the Small Business Administration, and publications like the *Wall Street Journal* and *Business Week.* Incidentally, the *Wall Street Journal* carries many valuable classified ads that are of definite interest to the Wealth-Base Builder. For example, there are always active lists of people and companies interested in investing money in new ventures. They also carry ads of businesses for sale, something you might consider either as a start, or to diversify your already growing business. Your local library—and the librarian—are often excellent sources of information.

There are many other books available to the Wealth-Base Builder, and you should investigate those which are relevant to your individual problems. For example, if you are planning to start a business, but lack capital, or the sources from which to get it, we strongly recommend Tyler Hicks' book entitled *How to Borrow Your Way to a Great Fortune.* This book, published by Parker Publishing Company, tells you how to start with no money—that's right—no money at all—and build the capital you need to build a Wealth Base. Your local librarian can often make other useful suggestions here.

Talk to Suppliers.   If you are planning a business which must use the services of others, don't hesitate to pick their brains. If you will need a printer to do some mailing cards, stop in and tell him of your plans. Not only will he be able to give you the printing advice you need, but the chances are that he will be able to tell you of the experiences of others. After all, he is in a position to find out how well other people do when they start a new venture.

If you plan to do any advertising in local newspapers, or directories, ask them to send a sales representative around. These people have a wealth of information at their fingertips, and because they are trying to sell you something, they are often anxious to give you details of the successes and failures of other similar ventures. They can tell you what has worked . . . and what has not worked. The advertising salesmen are indeed good friends to have.

Talk to Competitors.   This bit of market research may seem somewhat unethical, but actually under our free-enterprise system, finding out what a competitor does, and doing it better is what insures that the customer gets the best break. When you talk

to such competitors, it is often possible to tell them that you plan
to do just what they are doing.

"How?" you ask.

Simple! Many businesses are very localized in nature. That is,
they serve a very small trading area, and a similar business started
10 miles away would have no effect. Under these circumstances,
proprietors are often most willing to tell of their successes and failures.

If you are planning a mail-order operation, be sure to read
every possible magazine that carries ads for similar products and
services . . . and write to every advertiser for his pitch. After all, if
someone has been successful, you might as well try to improve on
his offer. You and your customers will be the winners.

Talk to Your Customers.   Let's say that you have the idea that
you can make money in the industrial food service, as we described it in this book. You had better talk first to your potential
customers before you invest a dime. There may be fifty factories in
your area, all with hundreds of hungry men, but you'd better find
out if they will buy your food. Many businesses have been started
with what appeared to be great potential, but because the proprietor neglected to talk to his potential customers first, the business
failed.

When you do ask questions, be direct. Don't be afraid to ask
prospects if they would buy. It is better to find out that you don't
have a market while things are still in the talking stage.

Businesses usually take longer to get in the black ink than
planned. If you have taken the time to make sure that you have a
market by talking to your suppliers, your competitors, and your
customers first, you will have the courage to sweat-it-out until it
goes. But, if you do not have any of these answers, and the going
is slow, there is often the temptation to abandon ship just before
things turn profitable.

Set Realistic Goals.   There is no better way to get things moving, and to guarantee success than to set goals, and put them in
writing. We're going to give you a timetable that most successful
businessmen have used, and that you can use to Build your
Wealth Base. But, you must stick to it to be effective. Here it is:

  1. Find the need that you want to satisfy. Write it down, and
     then begin to investigate the various businesses that you
     can start to satisfy this need.

2. Estimate the number of customers you will have for your business. Two excellent booklets, both available from the Small Business Administration will go a long way to helping you with this task: Marketing Planning Guidelines (Number 194), and Marketing Research Procedures (Number 9), both available at no cost.

3. Try to estimate what profit you can make with your product, or service, based on the number of customers you have estimated.

4. Decide how much time it will take to run the business. Here you must decide whether your business can be run as a part time venture, or if it will take a full-time effort to get it off the ground.

5. Make a careful analysis of the amount of money you will need. Three other SBA booklets are of immeasurable help. They are: Analyzing Your Cost of Marketing (Number 85), What Is the Best Selling Price (Number 193), and Is Your Cash Supply Adequate? (Number 174)

6. Find a place to operate the business. If you can start it at home, all the better. Again, profit by the experience of others. Check to see if similar businesses in your town are now being operated.

7. You now should have enough information on hand so that you can go thru the exercise of a trial run. Using the data you have collected, estimate your monthly cost of operation, and your monthly income, and see if you will be making a profit. Remember, if you have any large investment cost, you will seldom amortize them in a short run. At this point, it might be wise to seek the advice of a competent accountant. With the data you have collected, he can show you if and when you should have a money-making situation. And, too, he can often point out potential problems that you might have missed. After all, you will be very close to the business, and an outsider, unbiased in opinion will often save much time, money and heartache.

8. If everything checks out at this point, the chances are that you have a good potential business. The next step is to do it.

Once you have reached the point where all systems are "GO," you must keep these money making success tips in mind constantly:

1. *Stick with it.* Very few businesses were built overnight. If all the indicators say that your business will succeed, the only other success factor that really counts is perseverance.
2. *Be willing to take a chance.* We don't mean be reckless, but you must be willing to go out on a limb once in a while. It is the person who tries, fails, and goes on again that makes it. You must be willing to make mistakes, and to consider them to be learning experiences. For one thing, you will never repeat a mistake. For another, most mistakes point the way to the correct way of doing things.
3. *Don't be blind to other opportunities.* Many a businessman has gone down the drain because he had fixed ideas, and wasn't willing to make changes when they became necessary. After all, many people went on making buggy whips after the automobile was a proven success.
4. *Be imaginative.* Be on the lookout for new, and better ways of running your business. Keep looking for ways to simplify your operation, and to add to your profit picture. Add new products and services that you can sell to the customers you already have. This last notion is the cornerstone of good business, and is particularly important if you are at all involved in any kind of mail order operation.
5. *Don't be afraid to borrow money to expand.* We have showed you how to take $100 and turn it into a Wealth Base, but there will come a time when you must seek outside financing. Tyler Hicks' book, already mentioned, is about the best source of information on this subject. Another up-to-date source of information on how and where to borrow capital is the *Business Guide and Capital Source Directory.* It is available from the James Peter Press, Box 571, Westwood, New Jersey 07675. The $10 price includes several special sections of value to every Wealth-Base Builder.
6. *Take a chance with new ideas.* Now is the time to tinker with that pet idea of yours. If it works, you'll have the capital to make it go. And, if it doesn't you will not be wiped out.

PERSONAL PRACTICES FOR
THE WEALTH-BASE BUILDER

Making a lot of money is as easy as A-B-C, as you have seen from this book. But, there is more to doing it than simply following a list of formulas. You are a person, an individual, and you must build your business to suit not only your needs, but your very personality. And, you must be aware that most businesses demand more of the individual than the work of being someone else's employee.

At all times, keep your Wealth Base clearly in view. Make your daily activity a part of this quest. Keep tuned in to the little opportunities that pass right by the wage-slave.

If you are to succeed in building a Wealth Base, you must acquire an almost dogged determination. You should set your schedule so that you accomplish something every day. Set your daily goals high, and make sure that nothing interferes with them. We are not advocating that you shut off the world, but we are saying that you must set a definite schedule of activity and keep to it. If you must look at that football game, make sure that you will have a few hours available—that same day—to accomplish something for your business. Putting things off is the curse of the beginning Wealth-Base Builder.

This kind of activity is foreign to most people who never operated their own business, and often it is enough to turn them off before things get rolling. But, for the person who sticks to it, the ultimate freedom and riches are more than adequate compensation.

MAKE USE OF ALL YOUR TALENTS

When you work for someone else, the chances are that you do about the same thing every day. After all, that is the strength of the large corporations—a lot of skilled people doing their own specialized kind of work. But, as the owner of your own business, you will be called upon to do just about everything. We can't tell you the satisfaction you'll get from this. At first, you may feel overwhelmed, but it's the best training you can get. All the courses in business colleges never prepare the businessman for this kind of activity. And, once you have learned all the ins-and-outs of your business, you will have no fears of hiring people to take on specific areas of work. After all, you will know, in detail, just what is going on, and can become the true manager that you must be to really make big money.

INVEST TIME FIRST . . . THEN MONEY

The title of this chapter is "Don't Re-Invent the Wheel." What we have been saying is this: do your ground work carefully, make sure that there is a need for the business, and that you can successfully satisfy the need for your own profit. If you are selling several products and services, be sure that each produces its own share of the profit.

If, for example, you are selling a product that nets you a 22% profit and one that nets 5%, you must analyze the situation carefully. How many of each are you selling, and would it be profitable to discontinue one to emphasize the other? These questions are important, and the advice of a business consultant, or CPA should be sought. There is one business secret that we cannot emphasize too strongly here, and it is this:

> • Emphasize those products and services that make the most money for you. Anything that is less profitable can take time from your sales efforts, and drastically dilute your profits.

You can easily test the validity of this by "profiting by the experience of others." Visit a store that sells china, and tableware. Pick out the prettiest pattern, which is almost always that which is most prominently displayed, and the ugliest, which is usually relegated to a dark corner of the shop. Then ask the proprietor which he can deliver immediately. The chances are that he can give you immediate delivery on the prettiest, but you will have to wait for a shipment of the other. The reason for this is simple: He is doing a "volume" business in only a few of the more popular styles, and must move merchandise rapidly for a fast profit. He will seldom stock the ugly pieces because they take up space needed for the profitable merchandise. You might ask: "Why then, does he bother to stock something that doesn't sell?" This is a legitimate question, and the answer will be important if you are considering a business which must stock a range of styles.

Customers want to be able to make a choice. Even if you know that you will sell only the "beautiful" pieces, you must allow the customer to make his own selection. If you were to stock only those pieces which sell heavily, you would be out of business in a hurry.

To sum up what we have been saying, the fastest way to success is to profit by the experience of others. Plan carefully, and start your business with the understanding that it will take time before you can call it a success. After all, if businesses could be started over night everybody would be in business for themselves. The fact that you are reading this book indicates that you have the motivation to make a fortune, but do it carefully, and above all, profit by the experience of others.

5

Good Records Protect
Your Profits

The best time to start your business record keeping is *before* you earn a single dollar. Nobody likes the idea of paperwork, but it is vitally needed if you are to prosper in your new-found enterprise. Here are some of the reasons why you have to think about it right now:

1. There are tax, legal, and insurance angles to running a home business that can save or cost you money
2. You want to know for sure what kind of profit you are *really* making. Good record keeping can help you plug profit leaks
3. Once you get to the point that you decide to take a "giant step" forward in your business, you'll need good records to show banks or other investors.

You don't have to be an accountant or even have bookkeeping

knowledge to maintain a perfectly adequate set of records. Let's look at some of the things you should do at this point:

LEGAL AND TAX PROBLEMS

Registration.   Many towns and states have laws governing businesses. If you want to incorporate your business, you'll need a lawyer to draw up the various papers. It will probably cost you several hundred dollars. In the beginning, you should probably not consider incorporation, even though it has certain advantages as far as liability goes.

If you operate as a simple proprietorship, nothing very expensive or burdensome is required in registering your business. Check with your borough hall or county courthouse clerk and get the information you need. For a small fee, you can usually register your name and business. This will enable you to open a business checking account at your bank, and sometimes protect your company name if you want to incorporate later on.

Banking.   Open a business checking account as soon as possible. Apart from the prestige of having checks printed with your new business name, you will have taken the first step toward future growth. Every banker is pleased to get a new business account regardless how small it may be in the beginning. He is just as anxious for you to grow as you are. This is the ideal time to meet your banker and make friends.

All your transactions should be through this bank account. Deposit all earnings and pay all expenses with checks drawn on this account. It's a great temptation to pay cash for minor items you may use for business purposes, but a check will be absolute proof of expenses should the tax man ever question your tax return.

Insurance.   The next person you should talk to is your insurance agent. If you have any dealings at all with the public, particularly if you go into other people's homes, you should protect yourself with a liability policy. Fortunately, you can get a lot of coverage at relatively low rates.

If you use your own car for business purposes, you should tell that fact to your agent, also. It may mean a slight increase in premiums, but the peace of mind is worth it. If your policy is re-

stricted to pleasure driving and family use only, you might find
yourself without any coverage at all if you had an accident while
on business.

RECORD KEEPING

Provide yourself with a simple account book. In the beginning,
all you need do is to put all your income on one side, and all your
expenses on the other side. At the end of the month subtract your
expenses from your income and you can see your profit at a
glance.

You will also have to keep more careful household records if
you want to take advantage of all the tax benefits available to you.
A reasonable part of all the expenses of running your home are le-
gitimately deductible if you work from your home. How much depends on how much space you use in your home in the pursuit of
your business.

Your local office of the Internal Revenue Service has numerous
booklets available on various tax questions. Pay them a visit and
find out all the benefits possible. Your business can buy you a new
car; even though you use it for yourself and your family, a lot of
the expense of purchase and upkeep can be deductible because it
is used in your business.

Permanent Books.   If you keep careful records, saving all bank
statements, cancelled checks, bills, and the like, you should have
no trouble at income tax time. Once your business grows some
and you start acquiring equipment, the problems get a little more
complicated. You have to worry about things like depreciation
and the like. There are several ways you can handle this.

Elsewhere in this book we outlined the bookkeeping service for
business and the tax preparation service. If you want to do a fairly
professional job on your own books, then we suggest you look up
the references in those listed businesses. If you don't want to do
the job yourself, you can turn over the whole job to an outside accountant or bookkeeper. If your records are in order, it should be
very easy for an outsider to construct a simple set of books for you
and to maintain them at a very reasonable cost.

A Final Word.   Don't let the idea of record keeping scare you.

Most of your problems in the area will be eliminated if you are orderly. That means:

1. Have a safe place for all business records
2. Every bill, check, bank statement, and so on should go into this one place
3. At least once a month, go through your records and post them in your account book. Nothing is worse than trying to reconstruct financial records from missing parts, or scraps of information. Keep on top of the job!

Good records will tell you a story in a flash. You can see if you're not charging enough for your materials or your time. Good records will tell you what has to be changed for you to make your money goals.

Most of all—good records will impress your banker friend when you are looking for—say $50,000 or so—to invest in your business. What you do *now* will have a lot to do in whether he says "yes" at that time.

6

Now It's up to You

You can benefit from a second income in more ways than one. Obviously, you will have additional money. Obviously, you'll have all the luxuries and comforts money can buy—things like a new car, expensive vacations, a splendid new home, luxurious furnishings, fine clothes. But, if you will follow the simple, automatic steps we have outlined, you will be building a Wealth Base that can bring you even more. This is, literally, a base from which you can spring to great riches. You will have the capital and the experience you need to go on to the big money businesses that mean wealth and independence. Remember our magic formula:

C + C + C = Wealth

Capital plus *Credit* plus *Confidence* equals *Wealth.* You now will have all the essential ingredients to go on to build a fortune.

People who have built second-income fortunes have no more talent than you. They simply learned to use the 3-C formula, and observed the following principles:

- *Stick to it.* It's the accumulation of many small successes that add up to a beginner's fortune. By setting your sights on a goal, and not letting anything get in the way, you will be doing what every wealthy person has had to do to acquire his fortune.
- *Don't lose sight of your goal.* When the going gets rough— and it will—be sure that you don't lose sight of your goal. If you keep your goals firmly in mind, the going will be a lot easier—and quicker.
- *Be quick to make decisions.* We don't mean that you should act on a whim, but we do mean that you should size up an opportunity and move quickly. You will make mistakes. But, if you are decisive, you will make more correct choices than incorrect ones. When they are all added up, you will be way ahead of the person who hems and haws over a decision.
- *Keep an eye open to other opportunities.* Often, a beginning Wealth-Base Builder is so blinded by the small successes that come his way, that he misses important chances. You must be wary. You must be quick to seize opportunities, and to do this means that you must be flexible.
- *Be ready to borrow money when it is really needed.* Many businessmen never really make it because they are afraid to borrow the capital they need to turn a part-time venture into a full-time wealth producing business. Borrow wisely, though. Many a businessman has literally given his venture away because he didn't know how to borrow correctly. Ty Hicks' books, *How to Borrow Your Way to a Great Fortune,* published by Parker Publishing Company, is about the best source of information on this subject.

BEGIN Now—Set Your Goals and Decide What You Want.

By now, you have probably decided which of the businesses is for you. But, have you decided just what you want out of it?

- A big car
- A new home
- Money for travel

- A fine yacht
- Diamonds
- Mink coats

- Private schools
- Exclusive clubs
- Giant color TV

Whatever it is, put it down on paper right now. In fact, make a list of everything you would like to have. Then put the approximate value next to each item. Total it, and you have your FIRST goal.

You can now go back to the business you selected in the book, and see just what kind of money you can expect to make from it. Begin to work at it now, but do not let the lists of wants you just made be the end.

You will find that once you have gotten that fine car, the big house, the money for travel, they will all seem mere trifles. Now be able to afford things that were formerly only dreams. At this point, you make a new list. But, stick to the formula, and the principles we have outlined, and your income will approach that of a favored few.

Welcome, now, to the company of the wealthy!